COMMUNISM, THE COURTS, AND THE CONSTITUTION

Problems in American Civilization

UNDER THE EDITORIAL DIRECTION OF *George Rogers Taylor*

COMMUNISM, THE COURTS
AND THE CONSTITUTION

EDITED WITH AN INTRODUCTION BY

Allen Guttmann and Benjamin Munn Ziegler

AMHERST COLLEGE

Problems in American Civilization

D. C. HEATH AND COMPANY: Boston

INTRODUCTION

THIS problem concerns itself with people. Not any people, but people with ideas. Not any ideas, for that matter, but ideas which a preponderant majority hate, fear, and even consider inimical to their security. What shall be the status of such people? What rights do they have? And equally important, how shall this status and these rights be secured? This, indeed, is not a new problem. It is rather a recurring one and each generation must find, or help to find, its own answers.

Alexis de Tocqueville saw the problem as early as 1830 when he wrote about the possible "tyranny of the majority." For that matter the American people recognized it even earlier when they forced the Founding Fathers to add the Bill of Rights to the Constitution. And since that time our society has tried—from the passage of the Alien and Sedition Laws of 1789 to the Smith Act and McCarran Acts of the 1940's and 1950's—to deal with these people with these ideas.

The trouble with ideas is not so much that they stir up thought and even controversy, but rather that they tend to upset, potentially at least, the sense of basic value which forms the very foundations of society. Although a stock-taking or an inventory should be as valuable to a society as it is to a business, there are those who question the usefulness of a reassessment of values and ideas, who turn in anger on the proponents of reassessment, who seek to silence them with imprisonment or death. Galileo certainly found this to be true. What is apparently lost sight of is that, once stated, the idea or ideas themselves cannot be as easily imprisoned or buried as the people. As Max Lerner stated, "Ideas are Weapons." Mr. Justice Holmes went one step beyond and declared that "Every idea is an incitement," while at the same time Mr. Justice Brandeis cautioned that the way to deal with these ideas is with other ideas— "more speech, not enforced silence."

What is to be done then about people with ideas that "we loathe and believe fraught with death" depends to a large degree on what we desire. If we fear that radical change means chaos and the loss of liberty, if we hold—as does Wilmoore Kendall—that social order depends on a consensus and that all questions are *not* discussible, then prudence dictates one course of action. If, on the other hand, we believe that "time has upset many fighting faiths"; that "liberty is both an end and a means"; and that the "ultimate good desired is better reached by a free trade in ideas" since "truth is the only ground" on which a society of men can safely reach their goals, then the path must inevitably take a different direction.

These paths, while different, are not necessarily opposites. Nor are they created helter-skelter. They, like all paths that do lead somewhere, must be surveyed and marked out so that the meets and bounds will best conform to the conditions, purposes, and obstacles of time and place. The path that a democratic society like the United States attempts to mark out is predicated first of all on the proposition that it must have the inalienable right to defend itself against all enemies, domestic as well as foreign. The obstacle or condition it must take into account is that the fundamental law, the Constitution, provides for freedom of speech, press, assembly, and religion (First Amendment). If the surveyor be totally responsive to the will of the people, emotion, political overtones, sentimentality and the like will produce a path based on expediency and nothing else. If the surveyor be somewhat removed, somewhat in the position of Plato's "Philosopher-Kings," the path may not look as though it serves the needs of now but will, in the long run, more nearly reach the end desired in the first place.

We in the United States have sought the best of both theories. We have permitted Congress to respond to the will of the people (after it has, in many cases, created that will) by passing laws and, at least since *Marbury v. Madison* in 1803, have provided for judicial review of that response. So that in the final analysis Mr. Charles Evans Hughes was not completely wrong when he said: "The Constitution is what the judges say it is." This is all the more startling when one recalls that Alexander Hamilton, writing in Federalist No. 78, maintained "that the judiciary is beyond comparison the weakest of the three departments of power" since it "has no influence over either the sword or the purse . . . it may truly be said to have neither Force nor Will, but merely judgment."

Yet it is this very area of "judgment" that becomes the crux of the problem on three levels at once: the judgment of those who expound the ideas in the first place; the judgment of the elected representatives of the people as to how to deal with these ideas; the judgment of the Court as to which judgment should, in the final analysis, prevail. And as though this were not enough, it must be kept in mind that judges too are men with values and ideas, men who disagree with each other, men who, on occasion, show publicly their own private conflicts and inner indecision.

Perhaps the best that could be asked for in an imperfect world made up of imperfect men was stated by Judge Learned Hand:

"The judge's authority depends upon the assumption that he speaks with the mouths of others: the momentum of his utterances must be greater than any which his personal reputation and character can command; if it is to do the work assigned to it—if it is to stand against the passionate resentments arising out of the interests he must frustrate—he must preserve his authority by cloaking himself in the majesty of an overshadowing past, but he must discover some composition with the dominant trend of his times."

This book, from the clash of issues to its very end, asks one to see how well the Court has abided by that credo in dealing with the American Communists.

In Part I, the American Communists are permitted to speak for themselves. The selections chosen are representative in the sense that they express the official or semi-official position of the Party, and in the sense that they illustrate the major phases of the Communist Party in its history of nearly half a century. No attempt has been made to do justice to the opinion of *dissident* groups such as the Trotskyites, the Lovestoneites, and others who broke with the Communist Party and set up independent radical organizations.

The cases in Part II are illustrative of the many that have come before the Court. They have been chosen because they are the most important cases to date and because they may act as guideposts to the future direction the Court might take in this thorny area.

Part III offers commentary on both of the above to show, if nothing else, that this is not a problem simply of good versus evil, black versus white. The writers are not "straw men." They do not represent the "lunatic fringe" or provide the comments of the popular press. The essays are intended as aids for the serious student of a very complicated problem.

In the final analysis each reader must decide for himself what "path" should be followed; this in turn depends to a large degree on what the reader believes. Intelligent response or action cannot rely on the dictum that whatever is popular is true, anymore than it can push the hated and feared ideas under the rug by ridicule and scorn. If we agree that dogma and coercive force are not the final answers to heresy, if we are not ready to say that all problems are subject to the vicissitudes of political controversy and that the Courts, like everyone else, are, in the words of Mr. Dooley, "to follow the election returns," then we are thrown back upon argument, evidence, the rule of law, rational decision. What else is meant by the democratic slogan, "Let the people judge?"

CONTENTS

THE CLASH OF ISSUES

"The question in every case is whether the words used are used in such circumstances and are of such a nature as to create a clear and present danger that they will bring about the substantive evils that Congress has a right to prevent. It is a question of proximity and degree."

—MR. JUSTICE HOLMES in *Schenck v. United States*—249 U.S. 47 (1919)

"Men must be held to have intended, and be accountable for, the effects which their acts were likely to produce."

—MR. JUSTICE CLARKE in *Abrams v. United States*—250 U.S. 616 (1919)

"Freedom of press, freedom of speech, freedom of religion are in a preferred position."

—MR. JUSTICE DOUGLAS in *Murdock v. Pa.*—319 U.S. 105 (1943)

"I think the First Amendment, with the Fourteenth, "absolutely" forbids such laws [punishing utterances promoting friction among racial and religious groups] without any 'ifs' or 'buts' or 'whereases'."

—MR. JUSTICE BLACK, dissenting in *Beauharnais v. Illinois*—343 U.S. 250 (1952)

"The demands of free speech in a democratic society as well as the interest in national security are better served by candid and informed weighing of the competing interests . . . than by announcing dogmas . . . [and] primary responsibility for adjusting the interests which compete . . . belongs to the Congress . . . and the balance they strike is a judgment not to be displaced by ours, but to be respected unless outside the pale of fair judgment."

—MR. JUSTICE FRANKFURTER, concurring in
Dennis v. United States—341 U.S. 494 (1951)

I. THE COMMUNIST PARTY OF THE UNITED STATES

THE 21 POINTS OF THE THIRD INTERNATIONAL, 1920

As early as 1857, only nine years after the Communist Manifesto was issued, Conrad Carl, Siegfried Meyer and Friedrich Sorge organized, in New York, a Communist Club. In 1867, this club declared its membership in the International Workingmen's Association which Friedrich Engels and Karl Marx had founded in London in 1864. When Mikhail Bakunin threatened Marx's leadership of the First International in 1872, Marx transferred the headquarters of the organization to New York, where it expired four years later. Sorge presided over what one historian calls "the last rites and burial of the First International."* Marx's ideas were, however, kept alive within a number of organizations that began, flourished, withered, and died long before the Russian Revolution of 1917. From factions of the most important of these socialist organizations, the Socialist Party was founded in 1901 by Victor Berger, Eugene V. Debs, and Morris Hillquit.

The Socialist Party, which polled almost a million votes in 1920 (when Debs, its presidential candidate, was in jail!), adopted an evolutionary approach to socialism. Power was to be won through democratic processes rather than by revolutionary violence. This tradition of evolutionary socialism was maintained by Debs and has been continued by Norman Thomas until the present day. But not all socialists accepted the evolutionary brand of socialism. The International Workers of the World (IWW), founded in 1905, rapidly turned to violence under Daniel De Leon and William Haywood. And the Russian Revolution came to set an almost unbelievable example of the violent conquest of political power by a small group of determined revolutionaries.

The Socialist Party, which was badly split over America's entry into World War I, was further split by the formation of a "Left-Wing" movement that developed rapidly into two rival groups both anxious to affiliate themselves with Lenin's newly organized Third International. The Communist Labor Party and the Communist Party, both formed in the fall of 1919 from elements within the Socialist Party, differed on a number of issues, but not on their adherence to the principles of the Third International.

---

* Howard Quint, *The Forging of American Socialism* (Columbia: University of South Carolina Press, 1953), p. 3.

THE second congress of the Communist International adopts the following conditions for membership in the Communist International:

1. The entire propaganda and agitation must bear a genuinely Communistic character and agree with the program and the decisions of the Third International. All the press organs of the party must be managed by responsible Communists who have proved their devotion to the cause of the proletariat.

The dictatorship of the proletariat must not be talked about as if it were an ordinary formula learned by heart, but it must be propagated for in such a way as to make its necessity apparent to every plain worker, soldier and peasant through the facts of daily life, which must be systematically watched by our press and fully utilized from day to day.

The periodical and non-periodical press and all party publishing concerns must be under the complete control of the party management, regardless of the fact that the party as a whole being at that moment legal or illegal. It is inadmissible for the publishing concerns to abuse their autonomy and to follow a policy which does not entirely correspond to the party's policy.

In the columns of the press, at public meetings, in trade unions, in cooperatives, and all other places where the supporters of the Third International are admitted, it is necessary systematically and unmercifully to brand, not only the bourgeoisie, but also its accomplices, the reformers of all types.

2. Every organization that wishes to affiliate with the Communist International must regularly and systematically remove the reformists and centrist elements from all the more or less important posts in the labor movement (in party organizations, editorial offices, trade unions, parliamentary groups, co-operatives, and municipal administrations) and replace them with well-tried Communists, without taking offense at the fact that, especially in the beginning, the places of "experienced" opportunists will be filled by plain workers from the masses.

3. In nearly every country of Europe and America the class struggle is entering upon the phase of civil war. Under such circumstances the Communists can have no confidence in bourgeois legality.

It is their duty to create everywhere a parallel illegal organization machine which at the decisive moment will be helpful to the party in fulfilling its duty to the revolution.

In all countries where the Communists, because of a state of siege and because of exceptional laws directed against them, are unable to carry on their whole work legally, it is absolutely necessary to combine legal with illegal activities.

4. The duty of spreading Communist ideas includes the special obligation to carry on a vigorous and systematic propaganda in the army. Where this agitation is forbidden by laws of exception it is to be carried on illegally. Renunciation of such activities would be the same as treason to revolutionary duty and would be incompatible with membership in the Third International.

5. It is necessary to carry on a systematic and well-planned agitation in the country districts. The working class cannot triumph unless its policy will have insured it the support of the country proletariat and at least a part of the poorer farmers, and the neutrality of part of the rest of the village population. The Communistic work in the country is gaining greatly in importance at the present time.

It must principally be carried on with the help of the revolutionary Communist workers in the city and the country who have connections in the country. Renunciation of this work or its transfer to unreliable, semireformist hands is equal to renunciation of the proletarian revolution.

6. Every party that wishes to belong to the Third International is obligated to unmask not only open social patriotism, but also the dishonesty and hypocrisy of social pacifism, and systematically bring to the attention of the workers the fact that, without the revolutionary overthrow of capitalism, no kind of an international court of arbitration, no kind of an agreement regarding the limitation of armaments, no kind of a "democratic" renovation of the League of Nations will be able to prevent fresh imperialistic wars.

7. The parties wishing to belong to the Communist International are obligated to proclaim a clean break with the reformism and with the policy of the "center" and to propagate this break throughout the ranks of the entire party membership. Without this a logical Communist policy is impossible.

The Communist International demands unconditionally and in the form of an ultimatum the execution of this break within a very brief period. The Communist International cannot reconcile itself to a condition that would allow notorious opportunists, such as are now represented by Turati, Kautsky, Hilferding, Hillquit, Longuet, MacDonald, Modigliani, et al., to have the right to be counted as members of the Third International. That could only lead to the Third International resembling to a high degree the dead Second International.

8. In the matter of colonies and oppressed nations a particularly clear-cut stand by the parties is necessary in those countries whose bourgeoisie is in possession of colonies and oppresses other nations.

Every party wishing to belong to the Communist International is obligated to unmask the tricks of "its" own imperialists in the colonies, to support every movement for freedom in the colonies, not only with words but with deeds, to demand the expulsion of its native imperialists from those colonies, to create in the hearts of the workers of its own country a genuine fraternal feeling for the working population of the colonies and for the oppressed nations and to carry on a systematic agitation among the troops of its own country against all oppression of the colonial peoples.

9. Every party wishing to belong to the Third International must systematically and persistently develop a Communist agitation within the trade unions, the workers' and shop councils, the cooperatives of consumption and other mass organizations of the workers.

Within these organizations it is necessary to organize Communist nuclei which, through continuous and persistent work, are to win over the trade unions, etc., for the cause of Communism. These nuclei are obligated in their daily work everywhere to expose the treason of social patriots and the instability of the "center." The Communist nuclei must be completely under the control of the party as a whole.

10. Every party belonging to the Communist International is obligated to carry on a stubborn struggle against the Amsterdam "International" of the yellow trade unions.[1] It must carry on a most

[1] In 1919, The Social Democrats had reorganized, at Amsterdam, the International Federation of Trade Unions, a non-Communist group. [Ed.]

emphatic propaganda among the workers organized in trade unions for a break with the yellow Amsterdam International. With all its means it must support the rising international association of the Red trade unions which affiliate with the Communist International.

11. Parties wishing to belong to the Third International are obligated to subject the personnel of the parliamentary groups to a revision, to cleanse these groups of all unreliable elements, and to make these groups subject to the party executives, not only in form but in fact, by demanding that each Communist member of Parliament subordinate his entire activities to the interests of genuinely revolutionary propaganda and agitation.

12. The parties belonging to the Communist International must be built upon the principle of democratic centralization. In the present epoch of acute civil war the Communist Party will only be in a position to do its duty if it is organized along extremely centralized lines, if it is controlled by iron discipline, and if its party central body, supported by the confidence of the party membership, is fully equipped with power, authority and the most far-reaching faculties.

13. The Communist parties of those countries where the Communists carry on their work legally must from time to time institute cleansings (now registrations) of the personnel of their party organization in order to systematically rid the party of the petit bourgeois elements creeping into it.

14. Every party wishing to belong to the Communist International is obligated to offer unqualified support to every Soviet republic in its struggle against the counterrevolutionary forces. The Communist parties must carry on a clean-cut propaganda for the hindering of the transportation of munitions of war to the enemies of the Soviet Republic; and, furthermore, they must use all means, legal or illegal, to carry propaganda, etc., among the troops sent to throttle the workers' republic.

15. Parties that have thus far still retained their old Social Democratic programs are now obligated to alter these programs within the shortest time possible and, in accordance with the particular conditions of their countries, work out a new Communist program in the sense of the decisions of the Communist International.

As a rule the program of every party belonging to the Communist International must be sanctioned by the regular Congress of the Communist International, or by its executive committee.

In case the program of any party is not sanctioned by the executive committee of the Communist International, the party concerned has the right to appeal to the Congress of the Communist International.

16. All decisions of the Congress as of the Communist International, as well as the decisions of its executive committee, are binding upon all the parties belonging to the Communist International. The Communist International, which is working under conditions of the most acute civil war, must be constructed along much more centralized lines than was the case with the Second International.

In this connection, of course, the Communist International and its executive committee must, in their entire activities, take into consideration the varied conditions under which the individual parties have to fight and labor, and only adopt decisions of general application regarding such questions as can be covered by such decisions.

17. In connection with this, all parties

wishing to belong to the Communist International must change their names. Every party wishing to belong to the Communist International must bear the name: Communist Party of such and such a country (section of the Third Communist International). The question of name is not only a formal matter, but is also to a high degree a political question of great importance.

The Communist International has declared war upon the whole bourgeois world and all yellow Social Democratic parties. It is necessary to make clear to every plain workingman the difference between the Communist parties and the old official "Social Democratic" and "Socialist" parties that have betrayed the banner of the working class.

18. All the leading press organs of the parties of all countries are obligated to print all important documents of the executive committee of the Communist International.

19. All parties that belong to the Communist International, or that have applied for admission to it, are obligated to call, as soon as possible, but at the latest not more than four months after the second congress of the Communist International, a special convention for the purpose of examining all these conditions.

In this connection the central bodies must see to it that all the local organizations are made acquainted with the decisions of the second congress of the Communist International.

20. Those parties that thus far wish to enter into the Third International, but have not radically changed their former tactics, must see to it that two-thirds of the members of their central committees and of all their important central bodies are Comrades who unambiguously and publicly declared in favor of their party's entry into the Third International before the second congress of the Communist International.

Exceptions may be allowed with the approval of the executive committee of the Third International. The executive committee of the Communist International also has the right to make exceptions in the cases of the representatives of the center tendencies named in paragraph 7.

21. Those party members who, on principle, reject the conditions and those laid down by the Communist International are to be expelled from the party. The same thing applies especially to delegates to the special party convention.

Charles E. Ruthenberg: THE ENDS AND MEANS OF THE COMMUNIST PARTY

Charles E. Ruthenberg was born in Cleveland, Ohio, of devoutly Lutheran parents. He joined the Socialist Party in 1909 when his interest in theology led him away from rather than toward the ministry. He ran as a socialist for various public offices in Ohio and was, by 1917, the most important leader of the left wing of the Socialist Party. When the Communist Party was formed in 1919, he became its first national secretary. Although it is an exaggeration to say that he "was the founder of the Communist Party in the United States,"* it is true that, through the ins and outs of party politics in the 1920's, Ruthenberg maintained his position as one of the chief spokesmen for the Communist movement.

WHAT is the goal of the Communist Party? Wherein does it differ from other labor political parties? What is the rôle of the Communist Party—in this country the Workers' Party[1]—in the struggle for the emancipation of the workers? . . .

The communists accept as their guiding policy that the world imperialist war was the beginning of the decay and disintegration of the capitalist system. Although the capitalists, financiers, and statesmen have striven mightily since 1918 to find a solution to the financial and economic problems brought upon them by the war, the process of disintegration still goes on. At times there are slight improvements only to be followed by worse conditions. Financially and economically Europe draws nearer and nearer to the brink.

The communists point out to the working class that the capitalist system has outlived its day, that it cannot be re-

formed or reconstructed, that the misery and suffering which are the lot of the workers can only be ended by the workers establishing their rule and proceeding with the work of rebuilding the economic system on a communist basis.

The communists are under no illusion that this can be done over night. The struggle against the capitalist system may still last for decades, and even after the workers achieve power will go on for years. The communists do not attempt to deceive the workers by teaching them that the social revolution is a pink tea affair to be achieved in the legislative halls of the capitalist government. The lesson of the one country in which the workers have attained power —Soviet Russia—shows that after the workers' government is established, an iron dictatorship must rule as the instrument through which the struggle against the exploiters is carried forward there. The communists recognize the historic truth that no privileged class has ever given up its special position, its power to live in luxury through the exploitation of the oppressed class, without a

---

[1] From 1921 through 1923, the Workers' Party was the legal parallel of the "underground" Communist Party. [Ed.]

* Jay Lovestone, introduction to *Speeches and Writings of Charles E. Ruthenberg* (New York: International Publishers, 1928), p. 14.

From Jay Lovestone, ed., *Speeches and Writings of Charles E. Ruthenberg* (New York: International Publishers, 1928), pp. 68-71, 74-77. Reprinted by permission of International Publishers Co., Inc.

bitter struggle in which it has resorted to every means within its power to retain its privileged position.

Everything points to the fact that the struggle against capitalism in Europe and America will not differ from the class struggles of the past and that the workers in the fight to emancipate themselves must be ready for this struggle.

In the United States the communists today are advocating as their chief immediate proposals the amalgamation of the trade unions into industrial unions and the formation of a Labor Party. While the communists in the United States are the leaders in the struggle to bring about amalgamation and the formation of a Labor Party, this does not mean that when this goal is achieved the task of the communists is at an end.

For the communists, the amalgamation of the trade unions into industrial unions and the formation of a Labor Party to fight the political battles of the working masses of this country are but the first steps toward the ultimate goal of the Workers' Government and the communist society.

When these means of struggle are achieved there will still remain for the communists the task of bringing to the masses of the workers of this country the realization that the struggle against capitalism must be a struggle to abolish the whole capitalist order. It must teach them that the problem which the working class faces under the capitalist system cannot be solved through ameliorative measures won in the legislative bodies of the capitalist government or through victories won in the fight on the industrial field for better wages and working conditions. The communists will still have the task of educating the working masses to the necessity of their establishing the rule of the workers in place

of the rule of the capitalists. They will still have before them the work of bringing to the masses of the workers and farmers the understanding that the existing capitalist government is an instrument for the service of the capitalists, that it cannot be the form of government through which the workers may rule, but must be supplanted by a government growing out of the experiences and struggles of the workers, that is, a Soviet government. The communists will still have before them the task of educating the working masses of this country to the need of their establishing Soviet government and with it the rule of the workers—the Dictatorship of the Proletariat—which will use the governmental power in the interest of the workers as openly as it is now used in the interests of the capitalists.

It is because, after the first steps in the United States in the form of the organization of a Labor Party and the amalgamation of the trade unions, there will still remain these great tasks, that there must be a Communist Party—a separate, distinct organization which will have in its ranks the best educated, disciplined, and most militant workers, such as the Workers' Party of America.

The role of this party is to be the battalion at the front leading the working class hosts—industrial workers and farmers—forward against the enemy in spite of all persecutions, in spite of the efforts of the capitalists to destroy it, until the victory of the workers is won. . . .

By what methods can we win leadership over and the support of a majority of the working class for our program of the proletarian revolution and the dictatorship of the proletariat?

There are two methods through which it might be conceived that this could be done. The first of these is the method of propaganda; that is, that we should present to the working class our indictment of the capitalist system, facts about the exploitation of the working class, the theory of surplus value, the class struggle and the materialist conception of history, and by publishing books, newspapers, pamphlets on the subject and through agitation at meetings, convert a majority of the working class to a belief in our analysis of the existing capitalist social order and the way in which the evils of this system can be abolished. This method of propaganda to win the support of a majority of the workers is the method which has been employed by the Socialist Labor Party.[2] It is the method now advocated by the Proletarian Party.[3] These organizations believe that through a theoretical presentation of the fundamental communist principles a majority of the working class can be won for the support of these principles and that some fine day the proletarian revolution will come about. Such a method, however, will never bring about the proletarian revolution. If we were to depend upon propaganda alone we could wait for another million years and there would be no proletarian revolution nor a dictatorship of the working class.

We must carry on educational work in our party. We must carry on educational work among sympathizers of our party. It is our task to educate as many workers as possible to an understanding of the fundamental principles of communism but we cannot rely upon that method alone to achieve the proletarian revolution.

---

[2] The Socialist Labor Party, organized in 1877, carried on the Marxist tradition of Daniel De Leon. The party is still in existence. [Ed.]
[3] A "splinter" party formed in 1920 by Michigan Communists. [Ed.]

The method which has been adopted by the Communist International and the communist parties the world over is quite a different method. The method of the communists is one of the things which distinguishes the Communist Party from previous working class organizations which have sought to bring about the proletarian revolution.

As communists we know that the capitalist system brings about continual conflicts between economic groups in the present social order. The wage workers come in constant conflict with the capitalists over questions affecting their daily lives. The workers desire higher wages. They want shorter hours of labor. They want improvement in their working conditions. Struggles over these questions and even broader questions grow out of the fundamental conflict of the wage workers and the capitalists. These conflicts are not matters of theory. They are hard, bitter, everyday struggles which decide the standard of living of the workers and their families.

Similarly the exploited farmers find themselves in conflict with the exploiters from day to day. The farmers struggle against the bankers who hold the mortgages on their land. They are in continual conflict with the marketing organizations to which they sell their products. Their interests are in opposition to those of the railroads which transport their goods. Thus both wage workers and farmers are engaged in a continual struggle with the capitalists.

The policy of the Communist Party is to associate itself with the workers in the everyday struggle. Communists fight with the wage workers and farmers in support of the demands which they make of the capitalists because it is in these struggles and through these struggles that the workers learn the character of the capitalist system, and there is developed the will to power of the workers, the determination to triumph over the enemy who exploits and oppresses them.

The everyday struggles of the workers create the most favorable condition for establishing the influence and leadership of the Communist Party. The workers learn by experience the character of the capitalist system. They learn by their experience in the struggle that the government under the capitalist system is merely an agency of the capitalists for maintaining the system of exploitation. They learn this, not through theoretical presentation and proof of the facts, but through the hard knocks of their experience with the capitalists and with the government which supports the capitalist system.

While fighting with the workers to realize their immediate demands against the capitalists, it is the part of the communists to point out to them at every stage of the development of the struggle that these immediate demands cannot solve their problems. Thus in the process of the struggle itself, the workers become more conscious of their class interests and of their class enemy. It is in the process of struggle that the revolutionary will of the workers develops, and through these struggles they are led step by step to the final struggle of the proletarian revolution.

MANIFESTO OF THE COMMUNIST PARTY
OF THE UNITED STATES, 1934

Under Lenin, the Soviet Union moved from "War Communism" to the much less radical "New Economic Policy" of 1921-1922. After Lenin's death in 1924, Stalin defended Lenin's policies against the proposals of Leon Trotsky. During this period of struggle for leadership of the Communist Party, Stalin's tendency was to condemn "deviations" to the Left. When Stalin, having vanquished Trotsky and his allies, turned to attack Nikolai Bukharin, it became necessary to denounce movements to the Right. The fiercest abuse was thrown at the democratic socialists, who were denounced as "social fascists" because their refusal to cooperate with the Communists "objectively" (the jargon is Communist) aided the Fascists of Germany and Italy.

Speaking to the Thirteenth Plenum of the Executive Committee of the Communist International (January 1934), Earl Browder insisted that the "fascist direction" of Franklin Roosevelt's New Deal had become "clear to the whole world." Whatever Browder's qualms about this line of argument, he was chiefly responsible for the manifesto issued by the Communist Party of the United States of America (CPUSA) at its Eighth Convention (April 1934).

To ALL WORKERS OF THE U.S.A.:

We speak to you in the name of 25,000 members of the Communist Party who elected the delegates of this Eighth National Convention; in the name of several hundred thousand workers who elected fraternal delegates from trade unions, unemployment councils, workers' clubs, fraternal societies; in the name of the miners, steel workers, metal workers, auto workers, textile workers, marine workers, railroad workers, whose delegates constitute a majority of this convention.

To you, the working class and toiling farmers of the United States, this Convention of workers addresses itself, to speak a few plain words about the crisis, and about the possibility of finding a way out.

The crisis of the capitalist system is becoming more and more a catastrophe for the workers and toiling masses. Growing millions of the exploited population are faced with increased difficulties in finding the barest means of livelihood. Unemployment relief is being drastically cut and in many cases abolished altogether. Real wages are being reduced further every month, and labor is being speeded up to an inhuman degree.

The vast majority of the poor farmers are slowly but surely being squeezed off the land and thrown on the "free" labor market to compete with the workers. The oppressed Negro people are loaded down with the heaviest economic burdens, especially of unemployment, denied even the crumbs of relief given to the starving white masses, and further subjected to bestial lynch law and Jim-Crowism. Women workers and housewives are especially sufferers from the crisis, and from the fascist movements to drive them out of industry. Millions of young workers are thrown upon the streets by the closing of schools and simultaneously are denied any chance to earn their living in the industries.

The suffering masses have been told to look to Washington for their salvation. Mr. Roosevelt and his New Deal have been decked out with the rainbow promises of returning prosperity. But the bitter truth is rapidly being learned that Roosevelt and his New Deal represent the Wall Street bankers and big corporations—finance capital—just the same as Hoover before him, but carrying out even fiercer attacks against the living standards of the masses of the people. Under Roosevelt and the New Deal policies, the public treasury has been turned into a huge trough where the big capitalists eat their fill. Over ten billion dollars have been handed out to the banks and corporations, billions have been squeezed out of the workers and farmers by inflation and by all sorts of new taxes upon the masses. Under the Roosevelt regime, the main burden of taxation has been shifted away from the big capitalists onto the impoverished masses.

The N.R.A. and the industrial codes have served further to enrich the capitalists by establishing fixed monopoly prices, speeding up trustification, and squeezing out the smaller capitalists and independent producers.

The labor provisions of the N.R.A., which were hailed by the A. F. of L. and Socialist leaders as "a new charter for labor," have turned out in reality to be new chains for labor. The fixing of the so-called minimum wage, at below starvation levels, has turned out in reality to be a big effort to drive the maximum wage down to this point. The so-called guarantee of the right to organize and collective bargaining has turned out in reality to be the establishment of company unions. The last remaining rights of the workers they now propose to take away by establishing compulsory arbitration under the Wagner Bill, camouflaged as an attempt to guarantee workers' rights. Roosevelt has given official governmental status to the company unions, in the infamous "settlement" in the auto industry. This new step toward fascism is announced as a "new course" to apply to all industries.

All these domestic policies are openly recognized as identical in their content with the measures of professed fascist governments. This rapid movement toward fascism in the United States goes hand in hand with the sharpening of international antagonisms and the most gigantic preparations for war ever before witnessed in a pre-war period. More than a billion dollars have been appropriated for war purposes during this year. A large proportion of this has been taken directly out of the funds ostensibly appropriated for public works. Hundreds of millions are being spent on military training in the so-called Civil Conservation Camps, run by the War Department.

The policies of the government in Washington have one purpose, to make the workers and farmers and middle classes pay the costs of the crisis, to preserve the profits of the big capitalists at all costs, to establish fascism at home and to wage imperialist war abroad. . . .

Only the Communist Party has consistently organized and led the resistance to the capitalist attacks. The enemies of the Communist Party try to scare away the workers and farmers from this struggle by shouting that the Communist Party is interested only in revolution, that it is not sincerely trying to protect the living standards of the masses. They do this in order to hide the fact that they, one and all, pursue the single policy of saving the profits of the capitalists, no matter what it may cost in degrading the living standards of the masses.

The Communist Party declares that wages must be maintained no matter what is the consequence to capitalist profits.

The Communist Party declares that unemployment insurance must be provided at the expense of capitalist profits.

The Communist Party declares that the masses of workers and farmers must not only fight against reduction in their living standards, but must win constantly increasing living standards at the expense of capitalist profits.

The Communist Party declares, if the continuation of capitalism requires that profits be protected at the price of starvation, fascism and war for the masses of the people, then the quicker capitalism is destroyed, the better. . . .

It is no accident that whenever a big strike movement breaks out, the capitalist press shrieks that it is due to Communist influence, and the A. F. of L. and Socialist Party leaders wail that the masses have got beyond their control.

It is true that all struggles for daily bread, for milk for children, against evictions, for unemployment relief and insurance, for wage increases, for the right to organize and strike, etc., are directly connected up with the question of revolution. Those who are against the revolution, who want to maintain the capitalist system, are prepared to sacrifice these struggles of the workers in order to help the capitalists preserve their profits.

Only those can courageously lead and stubbornly organize the fight for the immediate interests of the toiling masses, who know that these things must be won even though it means the destruction of capitalist profits, and who draw the necessary conclusion that the workers and farmers must consciously prepare to overthrow capitalism.

The crisis cannot be solved for the toiling masses until the rule of Wall Street has been broken and the rule of the working class has been established. The only way out of the crisis for the toiling masses is the revolutionary way out—the abolition of capitalist rule and capitalism, the establishment of the socialist society through the power of a revolutionary workers' government, a Soviet government.

The program of the revolutionary solution of the crisis is no blind experiment. The working class is already in power in the biggest country in the world, and it has already proved the great superiority of the socialist system. While the crisis has engulfed the capitalist countries—at the same time in the Soviet Union, where the workers rule through their Soviet power, a new socialist society is being victoriously built.

The Russian working class, from its own resources and its socialist system, restored the national economy which had been shattered by six years of imperialist war and intervention. It overcame the age-long backwardness of Russia and brought its industrial production to the first place in Europe, to more than three times the pre-war figure. It rooted out the last breeding ground of capitalism by the successful inclusion of agriculture in the socialist system. It completely abolished unemployment and tremendously raised the material well-being and cultural standards of the toiling masses. Upon the basis of its socialist system, the Soviet Union has become the most powerful influence for peace in an otherwise war-mad world.

Its victories are an unending source of inspiration and encouragement to the toiling masses of every country. They are the living example of the possibility of finding a way out of the crisis in the interests of the toilers. The experience of the victorious workers of the Soviet Union before, during and after the seizure of power, throw a brilliant light showing the path which must be followed in every land, the path of Bolshevism, of Marx, Engels, Lenin and Stalin.

In the same period of successful testing of the Bolshevik road in the Soviet Union, we have also the example of the results of the policies of the Socialist Parties of the Second International. The Socialist Parties stood at the head of the majority of the working class in Germany and Austria. The revolutionary upheavals of 1918 in these countries placed power in the hands of the Socialist Parties. Their leaders repudiated the Bolshevik road, and boasted of their contrasting "civilized," "peaceful," "democratic," "gradual transition to Socialism" through a coalition government together with the bourgeoisie on the basis of restoring the shattered capitalist system. To this end they crushed the revolution in 1918.

They followed the policy of "the lesser evil," supported the government of Bruening with its emergency decrees against the workers, disarmed the working class, led the workers to vote for Field Marshal von Hindenburg, and finally crowned their infamy by voting in the Reichstag for Hitler after having paved the way for fascism since 1918. In Austria they supported the Dollfuss fascist government as the "lesser evil," enabling Dollfuss to turn his cannon against the homes of the Austrian workers.

Their "civilized" methods opened wide the gates for the most barbarous regime in the modern history of Europe. Their "peaceful" methods gave birth to the most bloody and violent reaction. Their "democracy" brought forth the most brutal and open capitalist dictatorship. Their "gradual transition to socialism" helped to restore the uncontrolled rule of finance-capital, the master of fascism. The German and Austrian working class, after 16 years of bitter and bloody lessons of the true meaning of the policies of the Socialist Parties, of the Second International, have now finally begun to turn away from them and at last to take the Bolshevik path.

In every material respect, the United States is fully ripe for socialism. Its accumulated wealth and productive forces, together with an inexhaustible supply of almost all of the raw materials, provide a complete material basis for socialism. All material conditions exist for a society which could at once provide every necessity of life and even a degree of luxury for the entire population, with an expenditure of labor of three or four hours a day.

This tremendous wealth, these gigantic productive forces, are locked away from the masses who could use them. They are the private property of the small parasitic capitalist class, which locks up the warehouses and closes the factories in order to compel a growing tribute of profit. This paralysis of economy in the interest of profit, at the cost of starvation and degradation to millions, is enforced by the capitalist government with all its police, courts, jails and military.

There is no possible way out of the crisis in the interest of the masses except by breaking the control of the state power now in the hands of this small monopolist capitalist class. There is no way out except by establishing a new government of the workers in alliance with the poor farmers, the Negro people, and the impoverished middle class.

There is no way out except by the creation of a revolutionary democracy of the toilers, which is at the same time a stern dictatorship against the capitalists and their agents. There is no way out except by seizing from the capitalists the industries, the banks and all of the economic institutions, and transforming them into the common property of all under the direction of the revolutionary government. There is no way out, in short, except by the abolition of the capitalist system and the establishment of a socialist society.

The necessary first step for the establishment of socialism is the setting up of a revolutionary workers' government. The capitalists and their agents shriek out that this revolutionary program is un-American. But this expresses, not the truth, but only their own greedy interests. Today, the only Party that carries forward the revolutionary traditions of 1776 and 1861, under the present-day conditions and relationship of classes, is the Communist Party. Today, only the Communist Party finds it politically expedient and necessary to remind the American working masses of how, in a previous crisis, the way out was found by the path of revolution. Today, only the Communist Party brings sharply forward and applies to the problems of today that old basic document of "Americanism," the Declaration of Independence.

Applying the Declaration of Independence to present-day conditions, the Communist Party points out that never was there such a mass of people so completely deprived of all semblance of "the right to life, liberty and pursuit of happiness." Never were there such "destructive" effects upon these rights by "any form of government," as those exerted today by the existing form of government in the United States. Never have the exploited masses suffered such a "long train of abuses" or been so "reduced under absolute despotism" as today under capitalist rule. The "principle" which must provide the foundation of the "new government" mentioned in the Declaration of Independence is, in 1934, the principle of the dictatorship of the proletariat; the new form is the form of the workers' and farmers' councils—the Soviet power. The "new guards for their future security," which the workers must establish, are the installing of the working class in every position of power, and the dissolution of every institution of capitalist class rule. . . .

The Communist Party calls upon the workers, farmers and impoverished middle classes to unite their forces to struggle uncompromisingly against every reduction of their living standards, against every backward step now being forced upon them by the capitalist crisis, against the growing menace of fascism and war. The Communist Party leads and organizes this struggle, leading toward the only final solution—the establishment of a workers' government.

The establishment of a socialist society in the United States will be at the same time a death blow to the whole world system of imperialist oppression and exploitation. It will mark the end of world capitalism. It will be the decisive step towards a classless society throughout the world, towards World Communism!

Earl Browder: DEMOCRACY OR FASCISM

Browder was not happy with the attack on Roosevelt as a "social fascist." Fortunately for him, the Seventh Congress of the Communist International (August 1935) announced Stalin's newest "line," the attempt to form a coalition with the democratic powers and thus to stop the increasingly powerful forces of Fascism in Europe and in the United States.

Browder was an excellent spokesman for the "People's Front," as the Anti-Fascist coalition was dubbed. He had been born in Kansas and he traced his ancestry back to seventeenth-century British immigrants to colonial Virginia. During his leadership of the Party, his Kansas "twang" and his alleged spiritual kinship to John Brown of Osawatomie, rather than his apprenticeship in the Communist Labor Party, were emphasized. Browder's attempt to apply the theory of the People's Front to American society led him into some difficulties during the election of 1936, when Roosevelt ran against Lemke (Union Party), Landon (Republican Party), Thomas (Socialist Party), and Foster (Communist Party).

THE world is torn between two main directions of development: on the one hand stand those forces striving to maintain the rights and living standards of the masses in the midst of capitalist crisis and decay, and to maintain world peace; on the other side are the forces of fascism, striving to wipe out popular rights and throw the full burden of the crisis onto the masses, and driving toward a new world war.

The camp of fascism, of the war-makers, is mighty and menacing. It is headed by Hitler fascism, the most bloody and

From *The People's Front* (New York: International Publishers, 1938), pp. 19-25, 28-32, 35-36. Reprinted by permission of International Publishers Co., Inc.

bestial reaction the world has ever seen. It contains Mussolini, whose hands drip with the blood of Italians and Ethiopians alike. It includes the military-fascist government of Japan, which is carving a new empire out of the body of the Chinese people. In every capitalist country its forces are organizing, backed and inspired by the monopolists of finance capital, and, where not already in power, are preparing with all energy, ruthlessness, and demagogy, to seize control of government. In the United States, this camp is headed by the dominant leadership of the Republican Party, with its allies of the Liberty League, Hearst, Black Legion, Ku Klux Klan, Coughlin, and others.

The camp of progress and peace finds its stronghold in the Soviet Union, the country of socialist prosperity. To its banner are rallying all the growing armies of those who would resist fascism and war. Relying upon its mighty strength, the French people were able to gather in the great *Front Populaire*, which threw back the first assaults of French fascism and warded off the first threat of war by Hitler, and advanced the living standards of the masses and their organized strength. Seeing in it a powerful protector, the small nations of Europe whose existence is threatened, who find less and less assistance from the great capitalist powers, turn to the firm peace policy of the Soviet Union as their reliable refuge. Even those great countries ruled by the imperialist bourgeoisie, like the U.S.A., who for their own special reasons are not ready for war, who want to maintain the *status quo*, at least for a time, must turn, even though hesitatingly, toward collaboration with the Soviet Union. The oppressed nations look to it for inspiration and leadership. Within each capitalist country, all forces for peace, and especially the workers and farmers, are beginning to see in the policy of the Soviet Union the chief hope of peace and progress in the world.

There are voices which shout of the menace of fascism and war, even in radical and "revolutionary" phrases, but which cannot find anything to say about the mighty and growing forces for progress and peace. Such voices come from confusionists and panic-mongers, who consciously or unconsciously are the advance agents of fascism, spreading defeatism and demoralization among the masses, disarming them before the enemy.

It is possible to defeat the fascists and war-makers. It is possible to move toward progress, to maintain peace. But to do this requires that we recognize and make full use of all factors, even the smallest, that work toward this end, even temporarily. It requires a drive toward *one united international policy*, around which is rallied the growing armies of progress and peace. It requires the recognition of the role of the Soviet Union, and full utilization of this great power.

The confusionists and panic-mongers all have one common starting point for their defeatism, fatalism and hopelessness. They reject the Soviet Union as a great power for progress and peace; some of them, like the Trotskyists, are moved by definitely counter-revolutionary theories and hatreds; others, like Norman Thomas, because they are filled with doubts, reservations, hesitations, misconceptions. Wherever this influence, in whatever degree, prevails among the masses, there we have more division instead of more unity, more confusion instead of more clarity, more defeatism and demoralization instead of the growth of a militant united movement against fascism and war.

But the united People's Front is winning the masses more and more in every country. It is overcoming the demagogic slanders of the counter-revolutionists, it is dissolving the doubts and hesitations of the confused people. It must, it can, and it will win the majority of the toiling people of every country. . . .

There are two chief and opposite directions of possible development in American political life in the 1936 elections. All parties and groups must be judged by their relation to these two fundamental political tendencies. One stems from the most reactionary circles of finance capital, Wall Street; its direction is toward fascism and war. The fundamental aims of this camp can be summarized in five points:

1. Restore capitalist profits by cutting wages, raising prices, checking the growth of trade unions, subverting them, and eventually wiping them out; squeeze out the poor farmers from agriculture, transforming them into propertyless workers.

2. Wipe out social and labor legislation, balance the budget by eliminating unemployment relief, cutting taxes of the rich and throwing the tax burden onto the poor by means of sales taxes.

3. Remove all remnants of popular influence upon the government, by vesting all final power in the hands of an irresponsible judiciary—the Supreme Court; drive toward the curtailment and eventual destruction of democratic liberties and civil rights; create the storm troops of reaction, Black Legions, Ku Klux Klans, etc.

4. Seize control of all governmental machinery, moving toward a full-fledged fascist regime, in "American" and "constitutional" ways.

5. Develop extreme jingoistic nationalist moods among the masses; drive toward war under cover of "American isolation" and "neutrality"; support to and alliance with Hitler and other fascists, preparing the new world war.

The other chief direction of possible development, insofar as it becomes effective, moves and must move toward an opposite set of fundamental aims, which can be stated as follows:

1. Restore and raise the living standards of the masses, by higher wages, shorter hours, lower prices, extending the trade unions to the basic industries and all workers, through militant industrial unionism; secure the farmers in possession of their farms, with governmental help and guarantee of a minimum standard of life.

2. Consolidate and extend social and labor legislation, with guarantee of a minimum standard of life for all, financing this with sharply graduated taxes on incomes, property and accumulated surpluses, abolition of sales taxes, balancing the budget at the expense of the rich.

3. Curb the usurped power of the Supreme Court; maintain and extend democratic rights and civil liberties; dispersal of reactionary bands, abolition of the use of legal machinery to suppress the people's movements; extension of popular control over government.

4. Restore control of the government to representatives of the people's organizations, through a broad People's Front.

5. Unite with the peace forces of the whole world to restrain the war-makers, to keep America out of war by keeping war out of the world.

How do the various parties and groups stand in relation to these two opposite and fundamental sets of objectives?

The Republican Party, headed by Landon and Knox, is unquestionably representing the full reactionary program. William Randolph Hearst has formulated that program with greatest clarity, has pursued it with the most vicious and obstinate energy. Hearst named the Republican ticket already in August, 1935. Morgan, the du Ponts, Mellon, all the most reactionary circles of Wall Street, are fully behind Landon and Knox. The platform of the Republican Party, behind a thin smoke-screen of tepid liberalism, contains all the essentials of Hearst's program, including its demagogy.

The Communist Party declares without qualification that the Landon-Hearst-Wall Street ticket is the chief enemy of the liberties, peace and prosperity of the American people. Its victory would carry our country a long way on the road to fascism and war.

Roosevelt and his administration are trying to pursue a middle course between these two opposite fundamental directions of policy. On the one hand, they try to keep mass support by certain small concessions to the needs and demands of the people. On the other hand, they answer the pressure and attacks of the reactionary forces by greater concessions in that direction. Especially in the last year, Roosevelt's course has been a series of retreats before the offensive of reaction. His administration is allowing itself to be dragged more and more onto the path of Hearst.

The Communist Party declares that it is a fatal mistake to depend upon Roosevelt to check the attacks of Wall Street, or to advance the fundamental interests and demands of the masses of the people.

Where, then, can the people turn to find protection against the reactionary forces that assail them?

With full knowledge that the great majority are not yet prepared to turn to socialism, as represented either by the Socialist Party or the Communist Party,

we Communists come forward with an immediate program which the masses are ready to support, to point out the path along which the people can maintain and advance their fundamental interests and rights. That immediate program arises out of the five fundamental aims of the masses of the people (which I outlined as the opposite of the reactionary program), which is the program of a People's Front, a program for democratic rights, for prosperity and peace.

This is not a program of revolutionary overthrow of capitalism. It can be realized within the framework of the present economic system by a people's government backed by the organized masses, determined to fight to keep Wall Street and its fascism out of power. . . .

We must frankly face and answer the question as to why, if the Landon-Knox ticket is the chief enemy, we do not come out in support of Roosevelt as the practical alternative this year. When Major Berry of Labor's Non-Partisan League was asked by the newspaper reporters if he was inviting the Communists to go along in their support of Roosevelt, he answered: "Let their conscience be their guide." Well, we have consulted both our conscience and our understanding; both join in counseling rejection of any reliance upon Roosevelt to defeat the reactionaries. Let us be very clear on this question. Our answer is not dictated by dogmatic rejection in principle of the idea of supporting a bourgeois candidate under any and all conditions. Lenin long ago taught us that such doctrinaire policies are not revolutionary. He taught us when, how, under what conditions, Communists could not only vote for but even enter into alliances with bourgeois candidates and parties—as against a threatening attack of overwhelming reactionary forces. . . .

Applying [Lenin's] principles to the United States in 1936, we reach certain conclusions on which our policy is based. We will review some of these conclusions in detail.

First, workers are interested, it is not a matter of indifference to them, as to which of two bourgeois parties shall hold power, when one of them is reactionary, desires to wipe out democratic rights and social legislation, while the other in some degree defends these progressive measures achieved under capitalism. Thus, we clearly and sharply differentiate between Landon and Roosevelt, declare that Landon is the chief enemy, direct our main fire against him, do everything possible to shift masses away from voting for him even though we cannot win their votes for the Communist Party, even though the result is that they vote for Roosevelt. This is not an example of the policy of the "lesser evil," which led the German workers to disaster; we specifically and constantly warn against any reliance upon Roosevelt, we criticize his surrenders to reaction and the many points in which he fully agrees with reaction; we accept no responsibility for Roosevelt.

Second, while we are not indifferent to the practical result of the election, we cannot support Roosevelt even as a means of defending democratic rights and social legislation which are seriously threatened, because Roosevelt himself is either unwilling or unable to conduct a serious struggle to this end. He is retreating before the attacks of reaction within his own party, as well as from the Republicans. He is bound within the limits of the reactionary Southern landlord interests, which control the Solid South, base of the Democratic Party. He yields most to reaction when he has the most support from the Left; he fights reaction only to the degree that he thinks necessary to hold labor and progressive forces from breaking away. Therefore, even from the narrow viewpoint of using Roosevelt against Landon, it is absolutely necessary to build the independent organization of labor and progressive forces for independent action—the Farmer-Labor Party;[1] to support Roosevelt is to invite him to make even further retreats.

Third, in order to have an alliance with the liberal bourgeoisie against the reactionaries, to preserve democratic rights, it is necessary for the workers and their more permanent allies (farmers and impoverished city middle classes) to have their own independent party, which at the same time prepares and conducts the struggle toward socialism. The two sides of the struggle must be developed together, or both are lost in a swamp of opportunist confusion or a desert of sectarianism.

That is why we do not support Roosevelt, although we direct the main fire against Landon. We have nothing in common with the approach to this question of the socialists, of Norman Thomas. Our friend Thomas sees the world through peculiar spectacles; he cannot see the fascist direction of the Republican Party, but rather accepts at its face value the crudely-staged "liberalization" of its Cleveland Convention. He thus renders unwilling but nonetheless effective aid to Hearst's demagogy. At the same time he proclaims the main issue of this election is socialism, and says of Roosevelt that he is probably the best thing under capitalism, that "if you want reforms, better stick to Roosevelt." From

---

[1] Browder's references are to a *potential* Farmer-Labor Party ticket that never materialized. This hoped-for Farmer-Labor Party is not to be confused with the Farmer-Labor movements in Minnesota and Wisconsin in the 1920's. [Ed.]

these premises he concludes it is a matter of indifference to the workers as to what kind of regime results from the election. We must describe such confusion as nothing but opportunist sectarianism.

Fourth, we must clarify the question, is socialism the issue that will be decided in this election? The war-cry of the reactionaries is that Roosevelt's New Deal is socialism or even communism. Norman Thomas gave some aid to this idea in 1933, during the honeymoon of the New Deal. Carried away by his enthusiasm, he hailed it as "a step toward socialism," as "a revolution." Now he swings just as far in the opposite direction, and sees little difference between Roosevelt and Landon, even while praising Roosevelt's liberalism. We must declare Roosevelt's policies as not socialism, nor a step to socialism. He at most tries to smooth out some of the worst abuses of capitalism, in order to give it a longer life. The reactionary cry of "socialism" is directed to two ends: first, to alarm all people of property to stampede them toward fascism; second, to discredit socialism among the masses by identifying it with the failures of the New Deal.

Before the two major parties, "socialism" is not an issue, but merely a demagogic war-cry of reaction. For the broad masses also, socialism is not the issue today, but rather the issue is, whether to move on the reactionary road toward fascism, or to struggle to maintain democratic rights, living standards, and peace. For the Farmer-Labor Party movement the issue is not between socialism and capitalism, but whether to move on the reactionary or progressive roads. We Communists, throwing our lot in with the Farmer-Labor Party movement, agree to fight for the road of progress under capitalism, together with those who are not adherents of socialism as we

are; while at the same time we point out that the only final guarantee of progress is to abolish capitalism and move to socialism.

Thus, we conclude that the direct issue of the 1936 elections is not socialism or capitalism, but rather democracy or fascism. At the same time we emphasize, and will always emphasize, that a consistent struggle for democracy and progress leads inevitably, and in the not distant future, to the socialist revolution. . . .

Let us summarize this examination of parties and issues in the 1936 campaign.

1. The chief enemy of the peace, freedom and prosperity of the American people is the Republican Party and its reactionary allies. Defeat the Landon-Hearst-Liberty League-Wall Street alliance!

2. Roosevelt and his administration are retreating before the attacks of reaction and surrendering position after position to the main enemy. Stop the surrender of our rights and interests in Washington!

3. The Socialist Party, after breaking loose from its reactionary Old Guard, is moving into the backwater of doctrinaire sectarianism, drifting out of the mass currents of American life. Win the socialists for the people's united front, for the Farmer-Labor Party!

4. The Farmer-Labor Party is rapidly growing in states and localities, it is organizing itself on a national scale. Support the program and platform of the Chicago Farmer-Labor Party Conference, build the Farmer-Labor Party!

5. The Communist Presidential ticket is the only banner in the national elections rallying and organizing all the forces of the people against reaction, fascism and war, building the People's Front in the United States. Vote the Communist Presidential ticket!

Gus Hall: OUR SIGHTS TO THE FUTURE

Browder's leadership, despite challenges from William Z. Foster, continued through the two-year period of collaboration between the Soviet Union and the Nazis (1939-1941), and through the years of the Second World War. After the invasion of the Soviet Union by the Nazis in June 1941, Browder led the American Communists in their period of intense dedication to the war effort. When the Party was legally dissolved into the Communist Political Association (1944), Browder continued to dominate the movement. William Z. Foster's disagreements were more or less effectively suppressed until April of 1945, when Jacques Duclos of the French Communist Party published an attack on Browder in Cahiers du Communisme. *After this indirect sign of Stalin's disfavor, Browder was replaced by Foster who became the leader of the reborn Communist Party. On February 12, 1946, Browder was expelled from the Party.*

The change in leadership was a part of a change in policy which was, in turn, related to the coming of the Cold War and the most difficult relations between the United States and the Soviet Union to date. The Party fell upon evil days. By the time of Gus Hall's keynote speech to the National Convention of December 10, 1959, membership had been decimated as a result of the Russian thrust into Eastern Europe, the Berlin Blockade, the Korean War, the anti-Stalinist revelations of Khrushchev at the 20th Congress (1956), and the Hungarian Revolution. By 1959 the Party was badly divided, beleaguered by hostile legislation, and intent more upon survival than upon the conquest of power. It remains to be seen if the position taken by Gus Hall, one of the twelve defendants in the Smith Act trials begun in 1949, is one compatible with the present thaw in the Cold War and the current tendency toward some kind of rapprochement *between the Soviet Union and the non-Communist world. The Party's recent support of President Kennedy and President Johnson suggests that Hall's program is, indeed, compatible with such a rapproachement.*

THESE are turbulent times. We are living in a period when events move with great speed—when decades are at things. The movement of events today turbulence merely on the surface of things. The movement of events today is profoundly reshaping the world. It is basically altering the relationship of forces and is creating a constant succession of new, unprecedented situations.

And the pace of these changes grows faster as time goes on.

It is in the midst of these developments that our 17th Convention meets. During the next four days we will undertake, dispassionately and realistically, to appraise the state of affairs in the world and in our own country, and to chart our course for the momentous period which lies ahead of us. This is a difficult

Keynote Speech to the 17th National Convention, CPUSA; reprinted from *Political Affairs*, XXXIX (January, 1960), pp. 1-15 with permission of the New Century Publishers, Inc.

task, but it is also an exciting and enthusing task—and a rewarding one.

The scope and speed of events is dramatized with special force by the contrast between the atmosphere, surrounding circumstances and outlook of this convention and the corresponding features of the 16th Convention. That convention took place in the midst of confusion and bewilderment resulting from the revelations of the 20th Congress of the CPSU concerning the weaknesses and mistakes of the Stalin era. It took place amid the disorientation and questioning created by the Polish and Hungarian events.

That was a period when world tensions were on the upgrade, and when the Dulles policies of "brinkmanship" and "massive retaliation" were in the ascendency. It was the period of the Suez invasion.

It was a time when the Party was in the depths of a crisis in which its very life or death was a subject of intense debate. It was a time of the gathering of the Right opportunist and liquidationist forces for their assault on the Party, an assault reflecting the world-wide revisionist swing which developed under the pressures of bourgeois ideology and as a reaction to the "Left"—sectarian, dogmatic practices of the past.[1]

Finally, the convention took place when the Party was just emerging from the disruption created by the attacks on it under the Smith Act and other repressive measures of the period when McCarthyism was at its height.

Looking back on the situation of those days, it must be said that the 16th Convention, in spite of all its weaknesses, was a positive achievement.

That convention had before it two central problems: 1) whether or not there was a place for a Communist Party in the United States, and 2) whether such a party, under American conditions, could be a Marxist-Leninist party. Despite the difficulties of that period, the convention gave affirmative answers to those questions and laid the basis for the re-consolidation of our party. Those struggles were necessary, and they prepared the party to meet today's tasks.

As is true in all phenomena, the elements of change—of the new—were then already discernible. The McCarthyite hysteria had already begun to subside. The Supreme Court decision had opened the doors to a new stage of the school desegregation fight. The peace movement was beginning to move forward, with the development of the campaign against nuclear tests. And the painful re-examination and correction of the 20th Congress contained within themselves the seeds of a new clarity and cleansing, and of a new upsurge of the world Marxist-Leninist movement. All these developments, however, were then present only in embryo or in their initial stages.

How radically and unalterably different are the circumstances in which our 17th Convention meets! Our Party enters this Convention victorious over the elements of liquidationism and revisionism, and having in the main eradicated their twin evils—"Left"-sectarianism and dogmatism.

This is a convention which ends all "holding operations" and sets our sights to the future. It is a convention of advance, of progress. This is the first convention to take place in the era when the socialist forces of the world have attained dominance, and when the world

---

[1] The "Right" at the 16th Convention (CPUSA) of February 1957 was led by John Gates, editor of the *Daily Worker*. Defeated by William Foster and Benjamin Davis, Gates and many of his followers resigned from, or were expelled from, the Party. [Ed.]

peace forces, for the first time in history, are the most powerful voice and movement on the world scene. This convention is being held at a time when the portals of opportunity have been opened to a new era of mankind, free of the scourge of war.

And it is being held at a time when the decline in our ranks has been halted, when the morale and fighting spirit of our membership is on the upgrade, reflecting these new developments in the world. The factionalism which caused such tremendous damage and threatened the very existence of the Party has been defeated, though remnants of it still exist.

In view of all this, the goals and aims of this convention must be far higher, far in advance of those of the 16th Convention. The heart of the 16th Convention was the struggle against those who maintain that there was no place for a Communist Party. Today this question does not even exist. Rather the central question of this convention is: what is the role of the Party in this entirely new situation? How can it now move out into the broad stream of the peoples movement; how can it break the bonds of its isolation and become more and more effectively a factor in the life of our nation—in the growing movement for peace, in the struggle of the workers, the Negro people, the youth and other sections of the people. . . ?

. . . This is the beginning of a new era in the life of our nation, our people and our Party. And we must not only see but must clearly define the features of this new era.

These were born and matured in the era that is ended—the era to which Henry Luce gave the name "The American Century." That was the era of the unquestioned dominance of the American monopolies in the capitalist world, of continuous expansion and growth with apparently no serious challenge from any source. It was an era in which American capitalism reached unprecedented heights, in which the rest of the capitalist world, prostrated by the war, lay at the feet of American big business. It was the era of "positions of strength," of dictation to other countries and infringement on their sovereignty.

It was an era that produced such bombastic, arrogant "carrot and club" policies as "containment" and "rollback" of the socialist world, and of trade embargoes intended to strangle its economic development. It was an era when American military bases mushroomed all over the face of the earth, and when the coffers of the American trusts were swelled with the profits extracted from the peoples of Latin America, Asia and Africa. Truly, the "American Century" seemed quite real and impressive.

This was the America which molded and left its imprint on our living standards, our culture, our thinking and our attitude toward the rest of the world. This is the America we must understand if we are to grasp the developing new features of the America which is succeeding it.

Let us now take a closer look at the new and developing. First we must look at the position our nation occupies in the world.

The outstanding world phenomenon of today is the fact that the balance of strength is tipping decidedly in the direction of the socialist world. This is a development of profound importance to every capitalist country, but its impact on the leading capitalist stronghold, the bastion of world capitalism, is a virtually explosive one.

The roots of these new relationships lie in the emergence after World War II of not one but a *group* of socialist countries—a socialist sector of the world embracing fully one-third of its people. These countries, bursting onto the scene of history, have undergone a meteoric growth, and are today moving at a terrific pace in their industrial, scientific, social and cultural development. Within a matter of a relatively few years, these socialist countries, so recently looked upon as backward, bid to become the dominant economic force in the world, producing more than half of its total industrial output.

This is a fundamental change, whose ramifications basically affect all parts of the world. But it is not the only challenge which has developed to the position of American capitalism.

Thus, it coincides with the beginning of the end of the era of colonialism. One colonial country after another is breaking out of its bondage and setting forth on the path of independence and national freedom. Beginning in Asia and the Near East, this development is sweeping across Africa, and is now challenging the dominance of the United States in what has been its own preserve, Latin America. The revolutionary development in Cuba, and the courageous resistance of the Cuban people to American imperialist intervention, is an inspiration to the people's forces throughout this hemisphere. This growing bloc of newly liberated countries represents a powerful new force on the world scene. . . .

A third major development of this era is the economic revival of the other capitalist countries. These have repaired the ravages of the war, and have gone through an extended period of expansion and modernization of their productive facilities. Today they are able to compete with American capitalists in field after field in which American products once reigned supreme. The share of the United States in world capitalist production, once over 50%, is now closer to 40. And the dominance which previously seemed so unquestioned is increasingly being challenged.

Growing competition from abroad has greatly narrowed the trade surplus enjoyed by this country for a number of years, and this has contributed to a huge jump in the deficit in the balance of payments with other countries. The deficit first appeared in 1950, and for the next several years it averaged about a billion dollars a year. But for the past two years, it has totalled more than $7½ billion. And this has created a threat to the stability of the dollar which is causing American big business no small alarm. . . .

The distinction is also illustrated by the fact that half a dozen years ago the Western European countries were appealing to the United States to let down its trade bars, under the slogan of "trade, not aid." But today it is Undersecretary of State Dillon who travels to Europe to ask for more markets for American goods from these very same countries. . . .

This is the new world in which our country must make a place for itself. In a true sense of the word, the problem our people face is that of finding the least painful transition from the "American Century" to the new era of challenge, of peaceful coexistence.

The central expression of the "American Century" concept has been the cold war. But with the fading of this concept, the cold-war policies of "positions of strength" and "brinkmanship" have proven themselves increasingly bankrupt. In this, a major factor has been also the peace policies of the Soviet Union.

As a result, American big business has been compelled to begin a painful re-examination of its policies—in the words of Dulles himself, an "agonizing reappraisal"—and to take a more realistic approach to the situation in which it finds itself.

In this lie the reasons for the proposal by Eisenhower for an exchange of visits with Khrushchev, leading to the historic visit of Khrushchev to this country and its momentous consequences. Among these were the Camp David agreement that "all outstanding international questions should be settled not by the application of force but by peaceful means through negotiations," laying the basis for summit discussions, as well as for direct meetings between heads of states. Among them, too, are a number of immediate gains—the conclusion of an agreement for expanded cultural exchange, agreements for cooperation in nuclear research and for joint medical research projects, and, of great significance, the agreement between the nations regarding the Antarctic continent.

This represents a break in the direction of American foreign policy. How fast or how far it will move in this new direction depends on the American people and on the pressure they exert.

It is not by any means the end of the cold war. The Eisenhower Administration has not yet shown in practice either the will or the actions to guarantee that this is the direction our country will follow. It has recognized the need for a change, but there is no indication as to how far-reaching or complete that change will be. And the die-hard cold war forces, who are very powerful, have already launched a counteroffensive designed to regain the ground they have lost and to wipe out whatever advances toward peace have been won. This is something which must be taken very seriously. . . .

. . . We must see clearly the distinctive features of the fight for peace in the present period. In past years, we organized, conducted and led a campaign for peace, including the notable Stockholm Peace Appeal. We did so in the context of the fundamentally correct analysis that a danger of war existed, exemplified by Korea and later by Indo-China. Today we are again taking part in a campaign for peace, but in the context of a new analysis—again fundamentally correct—that lasting peace, total disarmament and peaceful coexistence are in the cards, that they are realizable goals.

Both are campaigns for peace, but under such different conditions. Are we not called upon, then, to think about *specific* tactics to meet the *specific* conditions that flow out of the difference in the specific situations surrounding them? The past drive was based on a negative development; this one is based on a positive development. The past drive took place in a situation in which the peace forces were growing but not yet dominant; this one takes place in a situation in which the peace forces are already the stronger. The past drive occurred in an atmosphere of jingoism and national chauvinism; this one is unfolding in an atmosphere in which the whole nation is discussing the banning of nuclear tests, total disarmament and peaceful coexistence. These factors should indicate to us the need for fresh, concrete thinking.

There is a general, over-all sentiment for peace. This sentiment has grown in intensity as the weapons of war have increased in destructiveness. And as the balance of world forces has shifted, so have the moods and thinking of the mass of Americans shifted toward peace. It is this over-all yearning and concern for peace that forms the foundation for a concerted mass crusade for survival. This crusade is, of course, of utmost importance, and we must devote our best energies and forces to it. However, this is not enough. Such a *general* crusade will not by itself secure lasting peace.

The fight for peace must be developed in more specific forms. Its mooring lines must be tied to the specific self-interest of specific sections of the people. The campaign for peace is directed toward saving our lives and our civilization from destruction. But it also brings with it certain immediate benefits for the people and—yes—for the industrialists it means immediate profits. It is in relation to this that we must develop the slogans and the campaign for total disarmament. . . .

A generation of the American people has grown up in and made a livelihood from an economy that in large measure has been supported and souped up by war orders. War economy has been accepted as a normal and necessary part of our economic system. This stands as a roadblock to a full mobilization of the forces for peace. As Comrade [Hyman] Lumer's report will show concretely, this is a false conception. We have the task of removing this roadblock.

During these same years of the arms economy, a body of thought has developed to the effect that the Negro people can break down the bars of discrimination in industry, housing and education only when our nation is either at war or preparing for war. Unfortunately, there has been an element of truth in this. But we must show clearly how disarmament and peace can be conducive to an atmosphere in which this struggle can more readily be won. Wars and war tensions bring with them a growth of chauvinism and jingoism, while peace is con-

ducive to an atmosphere of brotherhood and understanding. We must understand these special roadblocks to the movement for peace among the Negro people.

Many Negro workers are at the bottom of the seniority list. Therefore any cutback in production means unemployment for them. This is a definite challenge to us in working out a substitute for military production.

Similarly, we need to deal with other specific problems affecting the young people, women, the handicapped and the old workers. Generalities will not do.

Hence, while we take part in the general crusade for peace, we must understand that specific groups, because of specific interests, will start from and rally around narrower issues involved in the fight for peace. With some, unrestricted trade with the socialist countries will be the starting point, with others it will be the dangers of fallout. For still others, disarmament will be the point of greatest interest.

We must see the fight for peace realistically in all its many-sided aspects. At this point, the need is not for starting a peace movement from scratch. Such a movement is here. It expresses itself in a thousand ways and at a variety of levels. At this stage, it is above all expressed through the existing mass organizations of the people.

In a nation like ours, where almost everyone belongs to one or more mass organizations, this is a firm and certainly a broad base. Here is where we should be working to help build and elevate the peace movement. . . .

There is a close relationship between world developments and those on the domestic scene.

What is it that best describes our domestic situation as we enter the decade of the sixties? Is it tranquility, stability?

Are we moving on the path of unending growth and expansion? In spite of the present high level of production, these words do not fit the realities of life in our country. Rather, the state of affairs in our nation is better described as one of instability, uneasiness and hesitation.

What best describes the United States of the sixties is the growing catalog of serious problems, steadily becoming more aggravated, which are seeking solution. And what gives these developments such importance and seriousness is that they occur simultaneously with the developments on the world scene which we have described.

An outstanding new feature on the home scene is the development of automation, whose many ramifications and effects are now reaching into all aspects of our national life. Strictly speaking, automation is still an infant. But it is already throwing its weight around like a full-grown heavyweight.

A most striking evidence of its effects is the rise in unemployment in the successive postwar boom periods. In the peak boom year of 1953, following the 1948-49 slump, 2.9% of the labor force was unemployed. In 1956, the year of peak economic activity following the 1953-54 slump, the figure was 4.2%. In the present period, which follows the depression of 1957-58, unemployment has remained well above 5% of the labor force. In October, 1959 it stood at 6%. Speaking on this question, Senator Eugene McCarthy of Minnesota had the following to say: "This is far too high for a dynamic economy, but its effect could be managed if it were spread evenly throughout the economy. The fact is that unemployment has reached disaster proportions in certain regions and for certain age, racial and educational groups."

What these figures show is a reemergence, since the war, of the industrial reserve army on a growing scale. And in this, the displacement of workers through automation is playing a constantly growing part.

Automation, and the determination of the monopolies to clear the way for more rapid automation, is also largely at the bottom of the current drive to undermine working conditions in steel, on the railroads, on the waterfront, and in many other industries. It serves also as an instrument used by big business for the destruction of its small competitors and increased concentration of ownership and control. The slogan of big business has become "Automate or Die." And in the process, many do die. . . .

A second major feature of the home scene is the growing financial instability of the country. Our national debt is higher than it was at the end of the war, and is still rising. The taxpayers are saddled with a burden of interest now in the neighborhood of $9 billion a year and still going up. State and local debts have been going up by leaps and bounds and are at an all-time high. Private debt has multiplied several times during the postwar years. The burden of taxes has grown to impossible levels, yet government debts continue to rise. Prices have risen greatly since the end of the war and the value of the dollar has been steadily shrinking. The federal government is experiencing increasing difficulty in financing the national debt and borrowing more money. As one observer has remarked, the credit of the United States government, once considered the soundest in the world, is now becoming shaky. And because of this country's world role, these developments are having worldwide repercussions.

A third important feature is the chronic agricultural crisis. . . .

To these features, we may add the failure of our society to provide adequate housing, education and health facilities, whose lack grows more acute from year to year. There is also the growing stench of corruption and moral decay, which is penetrating every corner of American life. As one person expressed it, "Everybody is on the gravy train of payola these days—except the working people."

Affected by all these things in the sharpest measure are in the first place the 18 million Negro people, as well as the 5 million Mexican-American and the million or more Puerto Ricans in the United States. The slum housing and the ghettoes to which they are confined are becoming not better but steadily worse. They are the most severely affected by the unfair system of taxation, by rising prices, by unemployment and by the farm crisis.

This is the America we see as we enter the decade of the sixties. These are the realities of life on the home front, corresponding to those in the world situation. It is these realities of life to which this convention must apply itself, and with which the Party must deal.

How does America react to these developments? What are the different currents which are emerging? In what direction are the different groups moving? In short, how is America meeting the challenge?

American monopoly capital is reacting to the world situation with attempts to readjust, reassess and make changes in its foreign policy, to accommodate itself to present-day realities. This is most dramatically demonstrated by the proposal for the Eisenhower-Khrushchev exchange of visits. And this in turn has been one of the basic factors in opening up the new possibilities which now exist in the fight for peace.

Thus, we have on the one hand the beginnings of a readjustment of direction in the sphere of foreign policy. But on the other hand, monopoly capital has reacted to the developments at home in an opposite manner. On this front, it is developing a most far-reaching, concentrated drive against labor, whose aim is to deprive the unions of all economic and political power, and to place them under complete government domination and control. The drive is marked especially by the passage of the Landrum-Griffin Act, by the attack on the steel union, and by a rash of proposals for additional anti-labor laws, including the outlawing of major strikes. The scope of the attack is indicated by the fact that Adlai Stevenson, who seeks the Democratic presidential nomination, has added his voice to the demand for outlawing strikes. The fight against this drive is the central issue, and we must not permit it to be sidetracked by such peripheral issues as racketeering, corruption and undemocratic practices, important as these are.

Accompanying the anti-labor offensive is a drive against civil rights and civil liberties. The forces of reaction have succeeded in bogging down completely the implementation of the Supreme Court anti-segregation decision. They have wiped the names of a quarter of a million southern Negro voters from the registration lists. They have been able to intimidate the Supreme Court and to make it retreat from its position on anti-Communist laws and other repressive measures, affecting not only the rights of Communists but those of the entire American people. The situation has reached such proportions that a Harry Truman, who once had liberal pretensions, now makes speeches against liberalism.

The entire drive of big-business reaction is of such scope and nature as to make the overwhelming majority of Americans its victims. In this lies the key to our mass and united front policies.

The victims of this drive have begun to fight back, and to give expression to their protests, resentments and demands. This is the basic feature of the situation, which we must recognize despite the confusion, the waverings and the ups and downs which exist. . . .

The Negro people's movement has shown an upsurge in a number of fields. New independent political movements are making their appearance. New levels of organization and activity are developing among Negro trade unionists, as witnessed by the struggles they waged at the AFL-CIO and UAW conventions. Of major importance is the formation of the Negro Labor Committee on the initiative of A. Philip Randolph.

Among the youth, there are growing signs of rebellion against the lack of decent jobs and training facilities, against the McCarthyite intimidation which disgraces our educational institutions, against segregation, and against the corruption and lack of perspective emanating from the cold-war atmosphere and pressures. To a growing extent, youth are becoming active in the peace movement today.

And so it is, too, with other sections of the people.

All these movements and struggles are developing alongside of the peace movement, and are related and intertwined with it, so that the success of one is dependent on that in others. To give leadership and guidance to this complex of movements at their existing level is therefore the central mass task of the Party. The multiplicity of forms and levels of the unfolding of the people's resistance must become our primary concern. . . .

Our electoral policies and activities in 1960 constitute an extension of . . . a united front policy. In very specific forms, the American people must find ways, through candidates and campaigns, to advance the struggle for peace and peaceful coexistence and to halt the offensive of big business at home. Wherever possible, the gap between these two opposite directions of development should be bridged in candidates and programs. However, where this is not possible, we should not therefore limit our electoral activities. We must find ways of giving support to candidates who take a positive position on the peace issue, while opposing any support they may give to the big business offensive at home, and vice versa.

While giving priority to the peace issue, all the needs of the people must be fought for—wages, jobs, labor's rights, civil rights and liberties, social security, housing, health, youth needs, etc. It is essential to show the direct relationship between the cold war and vast military expenditures, and the social and economic needs of the people.

On the basis of such movements and in connection with the election campaign, efforts must be made to forge broad electoral unity *to oppose the chief candidates of reaction and the cold war* and to promote the nomination and election of *pro-peace, pro-labor and pro-civil rights candidates* for office at all levels, including trade unionists and Negro representatives. It is also necessary to nominate and elect representatives from other minority groups, Puerto Rican and Mexican-American.

Labor and the Negro people can no longer be satisfied by a small few from their own ranks in Congress and public office. This election must see a substantial number of labor and Negro candidates from the primaries through the final elections.

An imperative task is to make the Dixiecrats a major target of attack, to expose and isolate them and to defeat their reactionary Republican and Democratic Party allies in the North. In the Democratic Party, in the labor unions and Negro people's organizations, and in all organizations that support the Democratic Party, the demand often raised by liberal forces should be pressed with full force today, namely to *oust the Dixiecrats from the Democratic Party.* . . .

Our Party has traveled a difficult path —and this not only since the 16th Convention. The enemy has thrown wave after wave, both internally and externally, against us now for ten years. We can say with just pride that the Communist Party of the U.S.A. has come through the fires battered but intact. We have suffered defeats but in an overall sense we have matured, become steeled and tempered. . . . We can now turn all of our attention and energies to the mass tasks and political responsibilities we face.

II. THE SMITH AND THE McCARRAN ACTS

THE SMITH ACT, 1940

[Sections 2 and 3 of the Smith Act . . . provide as follows:]

SEC. 2: (a) It shall be unlawful for any person—

(1) to knowingly or willfully advocate, abet, advise, or teach the duty, necessity, desirability, or propriety of overthrowing or destroying any government in the United States by force or violence, or by the assassination of any officer of such government;

(2) with the intent to cause the overthrow or destruction of any government in the United States, to print, publish, edit, issue, circulate, sell, distribute, or publicly display any written or printed matter advocating, advising, or teaching the duty, necessity, desirability, or propriety of overthrowing or destroying any government in the United States by force or violence;

(3) to organize or help to organize any society, group, or assembly of persons who teach, advocate, or encourage the overthrow or destruction of any government in the United States by force or violence; or to be or become a member of, or affiliate with, any such society, group or assembly of persons, knowing the purposes thereof.

(b) For the purposes of this section, the term "government in the United States" means the Government of the United States, the government of any State, Territory, or possession of the United States, the government of the District of Columbia, or the government of any political subdivision of any of them.

SEC. 3: (b) It shall be unlawful for any person to attempt to commit, or to conspire to commit, any of the acts prohibited by the provisions of . . . this title.

SMITH ACT CASES

Dennis et al. v. United States

MR. CHIEF JUSTICE VINSON *announced the judgment of the Court and an opinion in which* MR. JUSTICE REED, MR. JUSTICE BURTON *and* MR. JUSTICE MINTON *join.*

PETITIONERS were indicted in July, 1948, for violation of the conspiracy provisions of the Smith Act . . . during the period of April, 1945, to July, 1948. The pre-trial motion to quash the indictment on the grounds, *inter alia,* that the statute was unconstitutional was denied,

. . . and the case was set for trial on January 17, 1949. A verdict of guilty as to all the petitioners was returned by the jury on October 14, 1949. The Court of Appeals affirmed the convictions. . . . We granted certiorari, . . . limited to the following two questions: (1) whether either

---

341 U.S. 494 (1951).

sec. 2 or sec. 3 of the Smith Act, inherently or as construed and applied in the instant case, violates the First Amendment and other provisions of the Bill of Rights; (2) whether either sec. 2 or sec. 3 of the Act, inherently or as construed and applied in the instant case, violates the First and Fifth Amendments because of indefiniteness. . . .

The indictment charged the petitioners with willfully and knowingly conspiring (1) to organize as the Communist Party of the United States of America a society, group and assembly of persons who teach and advocate the overthrow and destruction of the Government of the United States by force and violence, and (2) knowingly and willfully to advocate and teach the duty and necessity of overthrowing and destroying the Government of the United States by force and violence. The indictment further alleged that sec. 2 of the Smith Act proscribes these acts and that any conspiracy to take such action is a violation of sec. 3 of the Act.

The trial of the case extended over nine months, six of which were devoted to the taking of evidence, resulting in a record of 16,000 pages. Our limited grant of the writ of certiorari has removed from our consideration any question as to the sufficiency of the evidence to support the jury's determination that petitioners are guilty of the offense charged. Whether on this record petitioners did in fact advocate the overthrow of the Government by force and violence is not before us, and we must base any discussion of this point upon the conclusions stated in the opinion of the Court of Appeals, which treated the issue in great detail. That court held that the record in this case amply supports the necessary finding of the jury that petitioners, the leaders of the Communist Party in this country, were unwilling to work within our framework of democracy, but intended to initiate a violent revolution whenever the propitious occasion appeared. Petitioners dispute the meaning to be drawn from the evidence, contending that the Marxist-Leninist doctrine they advocated taught that force and violence to achieve a Communist form of government in an existing democratic state would be necessary only because the ruling classes of that state would never permit the transformation to be accomplished peacefully, but would use force and violence to defeat any peaceful political and economic gain the Communists could achieve. But the Court of Appeals held that the record supports the following broad conclusions: By virtue of their control over the political apparatus of the Communist Political Association, petitioners were able to transform that organization into the Communist Party; that the policies of the Association were changed from peaceful cooperation with the United States and its economic and political structure to a policy which had existed before the United States and the Soviet Union were fighting a common enemy, namely, a policy which worked for the overthrow of the Government by force and violence; that the Communist Party is a highly disciplined organization, adept at infiltration into strategic positions, use of aliases, and double-meaning language; that the Party is rigidly controlled; that Communists, unlike other political parties, tolerate no dissension from the policy laid down by the guiding forces, but that the approved program is slavishly followed by the members of the Party; that the literature of the Party and the statements and activities of its leaders, petitioners here, advocate, and the general goal of the

Party was, during the period in question, to achieve a successful overthrow of the existing order by force and violence. . . .

The obvious purpose of the statute is to protect existing Government, not from change by peaceable, lawful and constitutional means, but from change by violence, revolution and terrorism. That it is within the *power* of the Congress to protect the Government of the United States from armed rebellion is a proposition which requires little discussion. Whatever theoretical merit there may be to the argument that there is a "right" to rebellion against dictatorial governments is without force where the existing structure of the government provides for peaceful and orderly change. We reject any principle of governmental helplessness in the face of preparation for revolution, which principle, carried to its logical conclusion, must lead to anarchy. No one could conceive that it is not within the power of Congress to prohibit acts intended to overthrow the Government by force and violence. The question with which we are concerned here is not whether Congress has such *power,* but whether the *means* which it has employed conflict with the First and Fifth Amendments to the Constitution. . . .

We pointed out [in *American Communications Assn. v. Douds,* 339 U.S. 382 (1950)], that the basis of the First Amendment is the hypothesis that speech can rebut speech, propaganda will answer propaganda, free debate of ideas will result in the wisest governmental policies. It is for this reason that this Court has recognized the inherent value of free discourse. An analysis of the leading cases in this Court which have involved direct limitations on speech, however, will demonstrate that both the

majority of the Court and the dissenters in particular cases have recognized that this is not an unlimited, unqualified right, but that the societal value of speech must, on occasion, be subordinated to other values and considerations. . . .

The rule we deduce from these cases is that where an offense is specified by a statute in nonspeech or nonpress terms, a conviction relying upon speech or press as evidence of violation may be sustained only when the speech or publication created a "clear and present danger" of attempting or accomplishing the prohibited crime, e.g., interference with enlistment. The dissents, we repeat, in emphasizing the value of speech, were addressed to the argument of the sufficiency of the evidence.

[One of the most important cases] in which free speech was the crux of the conflict was *Gitlow v. New York,* 268 U.S. 652 (1925). There New York had made it a crime to advocate "the necessity or propriety of overthrowing . . . organized government by force. . . ." The evidence of violation of the statute was that the defendant had published a Manifesto attacking the Government and capitalism. The convictions were sustained, Justices Holmes and Brandeis dissenting. The majority refused to apply the "clear and present danger" test to the specific utterance. Its reasoning was as follows: The "clear and present danger" test was applied to the utterance itself in *Schenck* [Schenck v. U.S., 249 U.S. 47 (1919)] because the question was merely one of sufficiency of evidence under an admittedly constitutional statute. *Gitlow,* however, presented a different question. There a legislature had found that a certain kind of speech was, itself, harmful and unlawful. The constitutionality of such a state statute had to be adjudged by this Court just as it determined the constitutionality of any state statute, namely, whether the statute was "reasonable." Since it was entirely reasonable for a state to attempt to protect itself from violent overthrow, the statute was perforce reasonable. The only question remaining in the case became whether there was evidence to support the conviction, a question which gave the majority no difficulty. Justices Holmes and Brandeis refused to accept this approach, but insisted that wherever speech was the evidence of the violation, it was necessary to show that the speech created the "clear and present danger" of the substantive evil which the legislature had the right to prevent. Justices Holmes and Brandeis, then, made no distinction between a federal statute which made certain acts unlawful, the evidence to support the conviction being speech, and a statute which made speech itself the crime. This approach was emphasized in *Whitney v. California*, 274 U.S. 357 (1927), where the Court was confronted with a conviction under the California Criminal Syndicalist statute. The Court sustained the conviction, Justices Brandeis and Holmes concurring in the result. In their concurrence they repeated that even though the legislature had designated certain speech as criminal, this could not prevent the defendant from showing that there was no danger that the substantive evil would be brought about....

... Nothing is more certain in modern society than the principle that there are no absolutes, that a name, a phrase, a standard has meaning only when associated with the considerations which gave birth to the nomenclature.... To those who would paralyze our Government in the face of impending threat by encasing it in a semantic straitjacket we must reply that all concepts are relative.

In this case we are squarely presented with the application of the "clear and present danger" test, and must decide what that phrase imports. We first note that many of the cases in which this Court has reversed convictions by use of this or similar tests have been based on the fact that the interest which the State was attempting to protect was itself too insubstantial to warrant restriction of speech. . . . Overthrow of the Government by force and violence is certainly a substantial enough interest for the Government to limit speech. Indeed, this is the ultimate value of any society, for if a society cannot protect its very structure, from armed internal attack, it must follow that no subordinate value can be protected. If, then, this interest may be protected, the literal problem which is presented is what has been meant by the use of the phrase "clear and present danger" of the utterances bringing about the evil within the power of Congress to punish.

Obviously, the words cannot mean that before the Government may act, it must wait until the *putsch* is about to be executed, the plans have been laid and the signal is awaited. If Government is aware that a group aiming at its overthrow is attempting to indoctrinate its members and to commit them to a course whereby they will strike when the leaders feel the circumstances permit, action by the Government is required. The argument that there is no need for Government to concern itself, for Government is strong, it possesses ample powers to put down a rebellion, it may defeat the revolution with ease needs no answer. For that is not the question. Certainly an attempt to overthrow the Government by force, even though doomed from the outset because of inadequate numbers or power of the revolutionists, is a sufficient evil for Congress to prevent. The damage which such attempts create both physically and politically to a nation makes it impossible to measure the validity in terms of the probability of success, or the immediacy of a successful attempt. In the instant case the trial judge charged the jury that they could not convict unless they found the petitioners intended to overthrow the Government "as speedily as circumstances would permit." This does not mean, and could not properly mean, that they would not strike until there was certainty of success. What was meant was that the revolutionists would strike when they thought the time was ripe. We must therefore reject the contention that success or probability of success is the criterion. . . .

[In other cases than these, the courts] were not confronted with any situation comparable to the instant one—the development of an apparatus designed and dedicated to the overthrow of the Government, in the context of world crisis after crisis.

Chief Judge Learned Hand, writing for the majority [of the Court of Appeals, interpreted "clear and present danger"] as follows: "In each case [courts] must ask whether the gravity of the 'evil,' discounted by its improbability, justifies such invasion of free speech as is necessary to avoid the danger." . . . We adopt this statement of the rule. As articulated by Chief Judge Hand, it is as succinct and inclusive as any other we might devise at this time. It takes into consideration those factors which we deem relevant, and relates their significances. More we cannot expect from words.

Likewise, we are in accord with the court below, which affirmed the trial court's finding that the requisite danger existed. The mere fact that from the period 1945 to 1948 petitioners' activities did not result in an attempt to overthrow the Government by force and violence is of course no answer to the fact that there was a group that was ready to make the attempt. The formation by petitioners of such a highly organized conspiracy, with rigidly disciplined members subject to call when the leaders, these petitioners, felt that the time had come for action, coupled with the inflammable nature of world conditions, similar uprisings in other countries, and the touch-and-go nature of our relations with countries with whom petitioners were in the very least ideologically attuned, convince us that their convictions were justified on this score. And this analysis disposes of the contention that a conspiracy to advocate, as distinguished from the advocacy itself, cannot be constitutionally restrained, because it comprises only the preparation. It is the existence of the conspiracy which creates the danger. . . . If the ingredients of the reaction are present, we cannot bind the Government to wait until the catalyst is added.

Although we have concluded that the finding that there was a sufficient danger to warrant the application of the statute was justified on the merits, there remains the problem of whether the trial judge's treatment of the issue was correct. He charged the jury, in relevant part, as follows:

In further construction and interpretation of the statute I charge you that it is not the abstract doctrine of overthrowing or destroying organized government by unlawful means which is denounced by this law, but the teaching and advocacy of action for the accomplishment of that purpose, by language reasonably and ordinarily calculated to incite persons to such action. Accordingly, you cannot find the defendants or any of them guilty of the crime charged unless you are satisfied beyond a reasonable doubt that they conspired to organize a society, group and assembly of persons who teach and advocate the overthrow or destruction of the Government of the United States by force and violence and to advocate and teach the duty and necessity of overthrowing or destroying the Government of the United States by force and violence, with the intent that such teaching and advocacy be of a rule or principle of action and by language reasonably and ordinarily calculated to incite persons to such action, all with the intent to cause the overthrow or destruction of the Government of the United States by force and violence as speedily as circumstances would permit. . . .

If you are satisfied that the evidence establishes beyond a reasonable doubt that the defendants, or any of them, are guilty of a violation of the statute, as I have interpreted it to you, I find as a matter of law that there is sufficient danger of a substantive evil that the Congress has a right to prevent to justify the application of the statute under the First Amendment of the Constitution.

This is matter of law about which you have no concern. It is a finding on a matter of law which I deem essential to support my ruling that the case should be submitted to you to pass upon the guilt or innocence of the defendants. . . .

It is thus clear that he reserved the question of the existence of the danger for his own determination, and the question becomes whether the issue is of such a nature that it should have been submitted to the jury.

The first paragraph of the quoted instructions calls for the jury to find the facts essential to establish the substantive crime, violation of secs. 2(a) (1) and 2(a) (3) of the Smith Act, involved in the conspiracy charge. There can be no doubt that if the jury found those facts against the petitioners violation of the Act would be established. The argument that the action of the trial court is erroneous, in declaring as a matter of law that such violation shows sufficient danger to justify the punishment despite the First Amendment, rests on the theory that a jury must decide a question of the application of the First Amendment. We do not agree.

When facts are found that establish the violation of a statute the protection against conviction afforded by the First Amendment is a matter of law. The doctrine that there must be a clear and present danger of a substantive evil that Congress has a right to prevent is a judicial rule to be applied as a matter of law by the courts. The guilt is established by proof of acts. Whether the First Amendment protects the activity which constitutes the violation of the statute must depend upon a judicial determination of the scope of the First Amendment applied to the circumstances of the case. . . .

There remains to be discussed the question of vagueness—whether the statute as we have interpreted it is too vague, not sufficiently advising those who would speak of the limitations upon their activity. It is urged that such vagueness contravenes the First and Fifth Amendments. This argument is particularly nonpersuasive when presented by petitioners, who, the jury found, intended to overthrow the Government as speedily as circumstances would permit. . . . A claim of guilelessness ill becomes those with evil intent. . . .

We agree that the standard as defined is not a neat, mathematical formulary. Like all verbalizations it is subject to criticism on the score of indefiniteness.

But petitioners themselves contend that the verbalization "clear and present danger" is the proper standard. We see no difference from the standpoint of vagueness, whether the standard of "clear and present danger" is one contained in *haec verba* within the statute, or whether it is the judicial measure of constitutional applicability. We have shown the indeterminate standard the phrase necessarily connotes. We do not think we have rendered that standard any more indefinite by our attempt to sum up the factors which are included within its scope. We think it well serves to indicate to those who would advocate constitutionally prohibited conduct that there is a line beyond which they may not go—a line which they, in full knowledge of what they intend and the circumstances in which their activity takes place, will well appreciate and understand. . . . Where there is doubt as to the intent of the defendants, the nature of their activities, or their power to bring about the evil, this Court will review the convictions with the scrupulous care demanded by our Constitution. But we are not convinced that because there may be borderline cases at some time in the future, these convictions should be reversed because of the argument that these petitioners could not know that their activities were constitutionally proscribed by the statute. . . .

We hold that secs. 2(a) (1), 2(a) (3) and 3 of the Smith Act do not inherently, or as construed or applied in the instant case, violate the First Amendment and other provisions of the Bill of Rights, or the First and Fifth Amendments because of indefiniteness. Petitioners intended to overthrow the Government of the United States as speedily as the circumstances would permit. Their conspiracy to organize the Communist Party and to teach and advocate the overthrow of the Government of the United States by force and violence created a "clear and present danger" of an attempt to overthrow the Government by force and violence. They were properly and constitutionally convicted for violation of the Smith Act. The judgments of conviction are

Affirmed.

MR. JUSTICE CLARK *took no part in the consideration or decision of this case.*

MR. JUSTICE FRANKFURTER, *concurring in affirmance of the judgment.*

Few questions of comparable import have come before this Court in recent years. The appellants maintain that they have a right to advocate a political theory, so long, at least, as their advocacy does not create an immediate danger of obvious magnitude to the very existence of our present scheme of society. On the other hand, the Government asserts the right to safeguard the security of the Nation by such a measure as the Smith Act. Our judgment is thus solicited on a conflict of interests of the utmost concern to the well-being of the country. This conflict of interests cannot be resolved by a dogmatic preference for one or the other, nor by a sonorous formula which is in fact only a euphemistic disguise for an unresolved conflict. If adjudication is to be a rational process we cannot escape a candid examination of the conflicting claims with full recognition that both are supported by weighty title-deeds. . . .

In all fairness, the argument cannot be met by reinterpreting the Court's frequent use of "clear" and "present" to mean an entertainable "probability." In giving this meaning to the phrase "clear and present danger," the Court of Appeals was fastidiously confining the rhetoric of opinions to the exact scope of what was decided by them. We have greater responsibility for having given constitutional support, over repeated protests, to uncritical libertarian generalities. . . .

First.—Free-speech cases are not an exception to the principle that we are not legislators, that direct policy-making is not our province. How best to reconcile competing interests is the business of legislatures, and the balance they strike is a judgment not to be displaced by ours, but to be respected unless outside the pale of fair judgment. . . .

Second.—A survey of the relevant decisions indicates that the results which we have reached are on the whole those that would ensue from careful weighing of conflicting interests. The complex issues presented by regulation of speech in public places, by picketing, and by legislation prohibiting advocacy of crime have been resolved by scrutiny of many factors besides the imminence and gravity of the evil threatened. The matter has been well summarized by a reflective student of the Court's work. "The truth is that the clear-and-present danger test is an oversimplified judgment unless it takes account also of a number of other factors: the relative seriousness of the danger in comparison with the value of the occasion for speech or political ac-

tivity; the availability of more moderate controls than those which the state has imposed; and perhaps the specific intent with which the speech or activity is launched. No matter how rapidly we utter the phrase 'clear and present danger,' or how closely we hyphenate the words, they are not a substitute for the weighing of values. They tend to convey a delusion of certitude when what is most certain is the complexity of the strands in the web of freedoms which the judge must disentangle." Freund, *On Understanding the Supreme Court*, 27-28. . . .

Third.—Not every type of speech occupies the same position on the scale of values. There is no substantial public interest in permitting certain kinds of utterances: "the lewd and obscene, the profane, the libelous, and the insulting or 'fighting' words—those which by their very utterance inflict injury or tend to incite an immediate breach of the peace." . . . We have frequently indicated that interest in protecting speech depends on the circumstances of the occasion. . . . It is pertinent to the decision before us to consider where on the scale of values we have in the past placed the type of speech now claiming constitutional immunity.

The defendants have been convicted of conspiring to organize a party of persons who advocate the overthrow of the Government by force and violence. The jury has found that the object of the conspiracy is advocacy as "a rule or principle of action," "by language reasonably and ordinarily calculated to incite persons to such action," and with the intent to cause the overthrow "as speedily as circumstances would permit."

On any scale of values which we have hitherto recognized, speech of this sort ranks low. . . .

These general considerations underlie decision of the case before us.

On the one hand is the interest in security. The Communist Party was not designed by these defendants as an ordinary political party. For the circumstances of its organization, its aims and methods, and the relation of the defendants to its organization and aims we are concluded by the jury's verdict. The jury found that the Party rejects the basic premise of our political system—that change is to be brought about by nonviolent constitutional process. The jury found that the Party advocates the theory that there is a duty and necessity to overthrow the Government by force and violence. It found that the Party entertains and promotes this view, not as a prophetic insight or as a bit of unworldly speculation, but as a program for winning adherents and as a policy to be translated into action.

In finding that the defendants violated the statute, we may not treat as established fact that the Communist Party in this country is of significant size, well-organized, well-disciplined, conditioned to embark on unlawful activity when given the command. But in determining whether application of the statute to the defendants is within the constitutional powers of Congress, we are not limited to the facts found by the jury. We must view such a question in the light of whatever is relevant to a legislative judgment. We may take judicial notice that the Communist doctrines which these defendants have conspired to advocate are in the ascendancy in powerful nations who cannot be acquitted of unfriendliness to the institutions of this country. We may take account of evidence brought forward at this trial and elsewhere, much of which has long been common knowledge. In sum, it would amply justify a legislature in concluding that recruitment of additional members for the Party would create a substantial danger to national security. . . .

On the other hand is the interest in free speech. The right to exert all governmental powers in aid of maintaining our institutions and resisting their physical overthrow does not include intolerance of opinions and speech that cannot do harm although opposed and perhaps alien to dominant, traditional opinion. The treatment of its minorities, especially their legal position, is among the most searching tests of the level of civilization attained by a society. It is better for those who have almost unlimited power of government in their hands to err on the side of freedom. We have enjoyed so much freedom for so long that we are perhaps in danger of forgetting how much blood it cost to establish the Bill of Rights.

Of course no government can recognize a "right" of revolution, or a "right" to incite revolution if the incitement has no other purpose or effect. But speech is seldom restricted to a single purpose, and its effects may be manifold. A public interest is not wanting in granting freedom to speak their minds even to those who advocate the overthrow of the Government by force. For, as the evidence in this case abundantly illustrates, coupled with such advocacy is criticism of defects in our society. Criticism is the spur to reform; and Burke's admonition that a healthy society must reform in order to conserve has not lost its force. Astute observers have remarked that one of the characteristics of the American Republic is indifference to fundamental criticism. . . . It is a commonplace that there may be a grain of truth in the most uncouth doctrine, however false and repellent the balance may be. Suppressing advocates of overthrow inevitably will also silence critics who do not advocate overthrow but fear that their criticism may be so construed. No matter how clear we may be that the defendants now before us are preparing to overthrow the Government at the propitious moment, it is self-delusion to think that we can punish them for their advocacy without adding to the risks run by loyal citizens who honestly believe in some of the reforms these defendants advance. It is a sobering fact that in sustaining the conviction before us we can hardly escape restriction on the interchange of ideas.

We must not overlook the value of that interchange. Freedom of expression is the well-spring of our civilization—the civilization we seek to maintain and further by recognizing the right of Congress to put some limitation upon expression. Such are the paradoxes of life. For social development of trial and error, the fullest possible opportunity for the free play of the human mind is an indispensable prerequisite. The history of civilization is in considerable measure the displacement of error which once held sway as official truth by beliefs which in turn have yielded to other truths. Therefore, the liberty of man to search for truth ought not to be fettered, no matter what orthodoxies he may challenge. Liberty of thought soon shrivels without freedom of expression. Nor can truth be pursued in an atmosphere hostile to the endeavor or under dangers which are hazarded only by heroes. . . .

It is not for us to decide how we would adjust the clash of interests which this case presents were the primary responsibility for reconciling it ours. Congress has determined that the danger created by advocacy of overthrow justifies the ensuing restriction on freedom of speech. The determination was made after due deliberation, and the seriousness of the congressional purpose is attested by the volume of legislation passed to effectuate the same ends. . . .

Civil liberties draw at best only limited strength from legal guaranties. Preoccupation by our people with the constitutionality, instead of with the wisdom of legislation or of executive action, is preoccupation with a false value. Even those who would most freely use the judicial brake on the democratic process by invalidating legislation that goes deeply against their grain, acknowledge, at least by paying lip service, that constitutionality does not exact a sense of proportion or the sanity of humor or an absence of fear. Focusing attention on constitutionality tends to make constitutionality synonymous with wisdom. When legislation touches freedom of thought and freedom of speech, such a tendency is a formidable enemy of the free spirit. Much that should be rejected as illiberal, because repressive and envenoming, may well be not unconstitutional. The ultimate reliance for the deepest needs of civilization must be found outside their vindication in court of law; apart from all else, judges, howsoever they may seek to discipline themselves against it, unconsciously are too apt to be moved by the deep undercurrents of public feeling. A persistent, positive translation of the liberating faith into the feelings and thoughts and actions of men and women is the real protection against attempts to strait-jacket the human mind. Such temptations will have their way, if fear and hatred are not exorcised. The mark of a truly civilized man is confidence in the strength and security derived from the inquiring mind. We may be grateful for such honest comforts as it supports, but we must be unafraid of its uncertitudes. Without open minds there can be no open society. And if society be not open the spirit of man is mutilated and becomes enslaved. . . .

MR. JUSTICE JACKSON, *concurring.*

What really is under review here is a conviction of conspiracy, after a trial for conspiracy, on an indictment charging conspiracy, brought under a statute outlawing conspiracy. . . .

The Constitution does not make conspiracy a civil right. The Court has never before done so, and I think it should not do so now. Conspiracies of labor unions, trade associations, and news agencies have been condemned, although accomplished, evidenced and carried out, like the conspiracy here, chiefly by letter-writing, meetings, speeches and organization. Indeed, this Court seems, particularly in cases where the conspiracy has economic ends, to be applying its doctrines with increasing severity. While I consider criminal conspiracy a dragnet device capable of perversion into an instrument of injustice in the hands of a partisan or complacent judiciary, it has

an established place in our system of law, and no reason appears for applying it only to concerted action claimed to disturb interstate commerce and withholding it from those claimed to undermine our whole Government. . . .

I do not suggest that Congress could punish conspiracy to advocate something, the doing of which it may not punish. Advocacy or exposition of the doctrine of communal property ownership, or any political philosophy unassociated with advocacy of its imposition by force or seizure of government by unlawful means could not be reached through conspiracy prosecution. But it is not forbidden to put down force or violence, it is not forbidden to punish its teaching or advocacy, and the end being punishable, there is no doubt of the power to punish conspiracy for the purpose. . . .

MR. JUSTICE BLACK, *dissenting.*

At the outset I want to emphasize what the crime involved in this case is, and what it is not. These petitioners were not charged with an attempt to overthrow the Government. They were not charged with overt acts of any kind designed to overthrow the Government. They were not even charged with saying anything or with writing anything designed to overthrow the Government. The charge was that they agreed to assemble and to talk and to publish certain ideas at a later date: The indictment is that they conspired to organize the Communist Party and to use speech or newspapers and other publications in the future to teach and advocate the forci-

ble overthrow of the Government. No matter how it is worded, this is a virulent form of prior censorship of speech and press, which I believe the First Amendment forbids. I would hold sec. 3 of the Smith Act authorizing this prior restraint unconstitutional on its face and as applied.

But let us assume, contrary to all constitutional ideas of fair criminal procedure, that petitioners although not indicted for the crime of actual advocacy, may be punished for it. Even on this radical assumption, the other opinions in this case show that the only way to affirm these convictions is to repudiate directly or indirectly the established "clear and present danger" rule. This the Court does in a way which greatly restricts the protections afforded by the First Amendment. The opinions for affirmance indicate that the chief reason for jettisoning the rule is the expressed fear that advocacy of Communist doctrine endangers the safety of the Republic. Undoubtedly, a governmental policy of unfettered communication of ideas does entail dangers. To the Founders of this Nation, however, the benefits derived from free expression were worth the risk. They embodied this philosophy in the First Amendment's command that "Congress shall make no law abridging . . . the freedom of speech, or of the press. . . ." I have always believed that the First Amendment is the keystone of our Government, that the

freedoms it guarantees provide the best insurance against destruction of all freedom. At least as to speech in the realm of public matters, I believe that the "clear and present danger" test does not "mark the furthermost constitutional boundaries of protected expression" but does "no more than recognize a minimum compulsion of the Bill of Rights." . . .

Public opinion being what it now is, few will protest the conviction of these Communist petitioners. There is hope, however, that in calmer times, when present pressures, passions and fears subside, this or some later Court will restore the First Amendment liberties to the high preferred place where they belong in a free society.

MR. JUSTICE DOUGLAS, *dissenting*.

If this were a case where those who claimed protection under the First Amendment were teaching the techniques of sabotage, the assassination of the President, the filching of documents from public files, the planting of bombs, the art of street warfare, and the like, I would have no doubts. The freedom to speak is not absolute; the teaching of methods of terror and other seditious conduct should be beyond the pale along with obscenity and immorality. This case was argued as if those were the facts. The argument imported much seditious conduct into the record. That is easy and it has popular appeal, for the activities of Communists in plotting and scheming against the free world are common knowledge. But the fact is that no such evidence was introduced at the trial. There is a statute which makes a seditious conspiracy unlawful. Petitioners,

however, were not charged with a "conspiracy to overthrow" the Government. They were charged with a conspiracy to form a party and groups and assemblies of people who teach and advocate the overthrow of our Government by force or violence and with a conspiracy to advocate and teach its overthrow by force and violence. It may well be that indoctrination in the techniques of terror to destroy the Government would be indictable under either statute. But the teaching which is condemned here is of a different character.

So far as the present record is concerned, what petitioners did was to organize people to teach and themselves teach the Marxist-Leninist doctrine contained chiefly in four books: Stalin, *Foundations of Leninism* (1924); Marx and Engels, *Manifesto of the Communist Party* (1848); Lenin, *The State and*

Revolution (1917); *History of the Communist Party of the Soviet Union* (1939).

Those books are to Soviet Communism what *Mein Kampf* was to Nazism. If they are understood, the ugliness of Communism is revealed, its deceit and cunning are exposed, the nature of its activities becomes apparent, and the chances of its success less likely. That is not, of course, the reason why petitioners chose these books for their classrooms. They are fervent Communists to whom these volumes are gospel. They preached the creed with the hope that some day it would be acted upon.

The opinion of the Court does not outlaw these texts nor condemn them to the fire, as the Communists do literature offensive to their creed. But if the books themselves are not outlawed, if they can lawfully remain on library shelves, by what reasoning does their use in a classroom become a crime? It would not be a crime under the Act to introduce these books to a class, though that would be teaching what the creed of violent overthrow of the government is. The Act, as construed, requires the element of intent—that those who teach the creed believe in it. The crime then depends not on what is taught but on who the teacher is. That is to make freedom of speech turn not on *what is said,* but on the *intent* with which it is said. Once we start down that road we enter territory dangerous to the liberties of every citizen.

There was a time in England when the concept of constructive treason flourished. Men were punished not for raising a hand against the king but for thinking murderous thoughts about him. The Framers of the Constitution were alive to that abuse and took steps to see that the practice would not flourish here. Treason was defined to require overt acts—the evolution of a plot against the country into an actual project. The present case is not one of treason. But the analogy is close when the illegality is made to turn on intent, not on the nature of the act. We then start probing men's minds for motive and purpose; they become entangled in the law not for what they did but *for what they thought;* they get convicted not for what they said but for the purpose with which they said it.

Intent, of course, often makes the difference in law. An act otherwise excusable or carrying minor penalties may grow to an abhorrent thing if the evil intent is present. We deal here, however, not with ordinary acts but with speech, to which the Constitution has given a special sanction.

The vice of treating speech as the equivalent of overt acts of a treasonable or seditious character is emphasized by a concurring opinion, which by invoking the law of conspiracy makes speech do service for deeds which are dangerous to society. The doctrine of conspiracy has served diverse and oppressive purposes and in its broad reach can be made to do great evil. But never until today has anyone seriously thought that the ancient law of conspiracy could constitutionally be used to turn speech into seditious conduct. Yet that is precisely what is suggested. I repeat that we deal here with speech alone, not with speech *plus* acts of sabotage or unlawful conduct. Not a single seditious act is charged in the indictment. To make a lawful speech unlawful because two men conceive it is to raise the law of conspiracy to appalling proportions. That course is to make a radical break with the past and to violate one of the cardinal principles of our constitutional scheme.

Free speech has occupied an exalted position because of the high service it has given our society. Its protection is essential to the very existence of a democracy. The airing of ideas releases pressures which otherwise might become destructive. When ideas compete in the market for acceptance, full and free discussion exposes the false and they gain few adherents. Full and free discussion even of ideas we hate encourages the testing of our own prejudices and preconceptions. Full and free discussion keeps a society from becoming stagnant and unprepared for the stresses and strains that work to tear all civilizations apart.

Full and free discussion has indeed been the first article of our faith. We have founded our political system on it. It has been the safeguard of every religious, political, philosophical, economic, and racial group amongst us. We have counted on it to keep us from embracing what is cheap and false; we have trusted the common sense of our people to choose the doctrine true to our genius and to reject the rest. This has been the one single outstanding tenet that has made our institutions the symbol of freedom and equality. We have deemed it more costly to liberty to suppress a despised minority than to let them vent their spleen. We have above all else feared the political censor. We have wanted a land where our people can be exposed to all the diverse creeds and cultures of the world.

There comes a time when even speech loses its constitutional immunity. Speech innocuous one year may at another time fan such destructive flames that it must be halted in the interests of the safety of the Republic. That is the meaning of the clear and present danger test. When conditions are so critical that there will be no time to avoid the evil that the speech threatens, it is time to call a halt. . . .

I had assumed that the question of the clear and present danger, being so critical an issue in the case, would be a matter for submission to the jury. . . . Yet whether the question is one for the Court or the jury, there should be evidence of record on the issue. This record, however, contains no evidence whatsoever showing that the acts charged, *viz.*, the teaching of the Soviet theory of revolution with the hope that it will be realized, have created any clear and present danger to the Nation. The Court, however, rules to the contrary. It says, "The formation by petitioners of such a highly organized conspiracy, with rigidly disciplined members subject to call when the leaders, these petitioners, felt that the time had come for action, coupled with the inflammable nature of world conditions, similar uprisings in other countries, and the touch-and-go nature of our relations with countries with whom petitioners were in the very least ideologically attuned, convince us that their convictions were justified on this score."

That ruling in my view is not responsive to the issue in the case. We might as well say that the speech of petitioners is outlawed because Soviet Russia and her Red Army are a threat to world peace.

The nature of Communism as a force on the world scene would, of course, be relevant to the issue of clear and present danger of petitioners' advocacy within the United States. But the primary consideration is the strength and tactical position of petitioners and their converts in this country. On that there is no evidence in the record. If we are to take judicial notice of the threat of Communists within the nation, it should not be difficult to conclude that *as a political party* they are of little consequence. Communists in this country have never made a respectable or serious showing in any election. I would doubt that there is a village let alone a city or county or state which the Communists could carry. Communism in the world scene is no bogeyman; but Communism as a political faction or party in this country plainly is. Communism has been so thoroughly exposed in this country that it has been crippled as a political force. Free speech has destroyed it as an effective political party. It is inconceivable that those who went up and down this country preaching the doctrine of revolution which petitioners espouse would have any success. In days of trouble and confusion when bread lines were long, when the unemployed walked the streets, when people were starving, the advocates of a short-cut by revolution might have a chance to gain adherents. But today there are no such conditions. The country is not in despair; the people know Soviet Communism; the doctrine of Soviet revolution is exposed in all of its ugliness and the American people want none of it.

How it can be said that there is a clear and present danger that this advocacy will succeed is, therefore, a mystery. Some nations less resilient than the United States, where illiteracy is high and where democratic traditions are only budding, might have to take drastic steps and jail these men for merely speaking their creed. But in America they are miserable merchants of unwanted ideas; their wares remain unsold. The fact that their ideas are abhorrent does not make them powerful. . . .

Free speech—the glory of our system of government—should not be sacrificed on anything less than plain and objective proof of danger that the evil advocated is imminent. On this record no one can say that petitioners and their converts are in such a strategic position as to have even the slightest chance of achieving their aims. . . .

Vishinsky wrote in 1948 in *The Law of the Soviet State.* "In our state, naturally, there can be no place for freedom of speech, press, and so on for the foes of socialism."

Our concern should be that we accept no such standard for the United States. Our faith should be that our people will never give support to these advocates of revolution, so long as we remain loyal to the purposes for which our Nation was founded.

Yates v. United States

MR. JUSTICE HARLAN *delivered the opinion of the Court.*

WE brought these cases here to consider certain questions arising under the Smith Act which have not heretofore been passed upon by this Court, and otherwise to review the convictions of these petitioners for conspiracy to violate that Act. Among other things, the convictions are claimed to rest upon an application of the Smith Act which is

hostile to the principles upon which its constitutionality was upheld in *Dennis v. United States,* 341 U.S. 494.

These 14 petitioners stand convicted, after a jury trial in the United States District Court for the Southern District of California, upon a single count indictment charging them with conspiring (1) to advocate and teach the duty and ne-

354 U.S. 298 (1957).

cessity of overthrowing the Government of the United States by force and violence, and (2) to organize, as the Communist Party of the United States, a society of persons who so advocate and teach, all with the intent of causing the overthrow of the Government by force and violence as speedily as circumstances would permit. Act of June 28, 1940, Section 2 (a) (1) and (3), 54 Stat. 670, 671, 18 U.S.C. Sections 371, 2385. The conspiracy is alleged to have orginated in 1940 and continued down to the date of the indictment in 1951. The indictment charged that in carrying out the conspiracy the defendants and their co-conspirators would (a) become members and officers of the Communist Party, with knowledge of its unlawful purposes, and assume leadership in carrying out its policies and activities; (b) cause to be organized units of the Party in California and elsewhere; (c) write and publish, in the "Daily Worker" and other Party organs, articles on the proscribed advocacy and teaching; (d) conduct schools for the indoctrination of Party members in such advocacy and teaching; and (e) recruit new Party members, particularly from among persons employed in the key industries of the nation. Twenty-three overt acts in furtherance of the conspiracy were alleged.

Upon conviction each of the petitioners was sentenced to five years' imprisonment and a fine of $10,000. The Court of Appeals affirmed. . . . We granted certiorari for the reasons already indicated.

In the view we take of this case, it is necessary for us to consider only the following of petitioners' contentions: (1) that the term "organize" as used in the Smith Act was erroneously construed by the two lower courts; (2) that the trial court's instructions to the jury erroneously excluded from the case the issue of "incitement to action"; (3) that the evidence was so insufficient as to require this Court to direct the acquittal of these petitioners; . . . For reasons given hereafter, we conclude that these convictions must be reversed and the case remanded to the District Court with instructions to enter judgments of acquittal as to certain of the petitioners, and to grant a new trial as to the rest.

One object of the conspiracy charged was to violate the third paragraph of 18 U.S.C. Section 2385, which provides:

Whoever organizes or helps or attempts to organize any society, group, or assembly of persons who teach, advocate, or encourage the overthrow or destruction of any [government in the United States] by force or violence . . . [s]hall be fined not more than $10,000 or imprisoned not more than ten years, or both. . . .

Petitioners claim that "organize" means to "establish," "found," or "bring into existence," and that in this sense the Communist Party was organized by 1945 at the latest. On this basis petitioners contend that this part of the indictment, returned in 1951, was barred by the three-year statute of limitations. The Government, on the other hand, says that "organize" connotes a continuing process which goes on throughout the life of an organization, and that, in the words of the trial court's instructions to the jury, the term includes such things as "the recruiting of new members and the forming of new units, and the regrouping or expansion of existing clubs, classes and other units of any society, party, group or other organization." The two courts below accepted the Government's position. We think, however, that petitioners' position must prevail, upon principles stated by Chief Justice Marshall more than a century ago in *United States v. Wiltberger*, 5, Wheat. 76, 95-96, as follows:

The rule that penal laws are to be construed strictly, is perhaps not much less old than construction itself. It is founded on the tenderness of the law for the rights of individuals; and on the plain principle that the power of punishment is vested in the legislative, not in the judicial department. It is the legislature, not the Court, which is to define a crime, and ordain its punishment. . . .

The statute does not define what is meant by "organize." Dictionary definitions are of little help, for, as those offered us sufficiently show, the term is susceptible of both meanings attributed to it by the parties here. The fact that the Communist Party comprises various components and activities, in relation to which some of the petitioners bore the title of "Organizer," does not advance us towards a solution of the problem. The charge here is that petitioners conspired to organize the Communist Party, and, unless "organize" embraces the continuing concept contended for by the Government, the establishing of new units within the Party and similar activities, following the Party's initial formation in 1945, have no independent significance or vitality so far as the "organizing" charge is involved. Nor are we here concerned with the quality of petitioners' activities as such, that is, whether particular activities may properly be categorized as "organizational." Rather, the issue is whether the term "organize" as used in this statute is limited by temporal concepts. Stated most simply, the problem is to choose between two possible answers to the question: when was the Communist Party "organized"? Petitioners contend that the only natural answer to the question is the formation date—in this case, 1945. The Government would have us answer the question by saying that the Party today is still not completely "organized"; that "organizing" is a continuing process that does not end until the entity is dissolved.

The legislative history of the Smith Act is no more revealing as to what Congress meant by "organize" than is the statute itself. The Government urges that "organize" should be given a broad meaning since acceptance of the term in its narrow sense would require attributing to Congress the intent that this provision of the statute should not apply to the Communist Party as it then existed. The argument is that since the Communist Party as it then existed had been born in 1919 and the Smith Act was not passed until 1940, the use of "organize" in its narrow sense would have meant that these provisions of the statute would never have reached the act of organizing the Communist Party, except for the fortuitous rebirth of the Party in 1945—an occurrence which, of course, could not have been foreseen in 1940. This, says the Government, could hardly have been the congressional purpose since the Smith Act as a whole was particularly aimed at the Communist Party, and its "organizing" provisions were especially directed at the leaders of the movement.

We find this argument unpersuasive. While the legislative history of the Smith Act does show that concern about communism was a strong factor leading to this legislation, it also reveals that the statute, which was patterned on state anti-sedition laws directed not against Communists but against anarchists and syndicalists, was aimed equally at all groups falling within its scope. More important, there is no evidence whatever to support the thesis that the *organizing* provision of the statute was written with particular reference to the Communist Party. Indeed, the congressional hearings indicate that it was the "advocating and teaching" provision of the Act, rather than the "organizing" provision, which was especially thought to reach Communist activities. . . .

On the other hand, we also find unpersuasive petitioners' argument as to the intent of Congress. In support of the narrower meaning of "organize," they argue that the Smith Act was patterned after the California Criminal Syndicalism Act; that the California courts have consistently taken "organize" in that Act in its narrow sense; and that . . . it should be presumed that Congress in adopting the wording of the California Act intended "organize" to have the same meaning as that given it by the California courts. As the hearings on the Smith Act show, however its particular prototype was the New York Criminal Anarchy Act, not the California statute, and the "organizing" provisions of the New York Act have never been construed by any court. Moreover, to the extent that the language of the California statute, which itself was patterned on the earlier New York legislation, might be significant, we think that little weight can be given to these California decisions. . . .

We are thus left to determine for ourselves the meaning of this provision of the Smith Act, without any revealing guides as to the intent of Congress. In these circumstances we should follow the familiar rule that criminal statutes are to be strictly construed and give to "organize" its narrow meaning, that is, that the word refers only to acts entering into the creation of a new organization, and not to acts thereafter performed in carrying on its activities, even though such acts may loosely be termed "organizational." . . .

The Government contends that even if the trial court was mistaken in its construction of the statute, the error was harmless, because the conspiracy charged embraced both "advocacy" of violent overthrow and "organizing" the Communist Party, and the jury was instructed that in order to convict it must find a conspiracy extending to both objectives. Hence, the argument is, the jury must in any event be taken to have found petitioners guilty of conspiring to advocate, and the convictions are supportable on that basis alone. We cannot accept this proposition for a number of reasons. The portions of the trial court's instructions relied on by the Government are not sufficiently clear or specific to warrant our drawing the inference that the jury understood it must find an agreement extending to *both* "advocacy" and "organizing" in order to convict. Further, in order to convict, the jury was required, as the court charged, to find an overt act which was "knowingly done in furtherance of an object or purpose of the conspiracy charged in the indictment," and we have no way of knowing whether the overt act found by the jury was one which it believed to be in furtherance of the "advocacy" rather than the "organizing" objective of the alleged conspiracy. The character of most of the overt act which was "knowingly done in readily with "organizing" as with "advocacy." In these circumstances we think the proper rule to be applied is that which requires a verdict to be set aside in cases where the verdict is supportable on one ground, but not on another, and it is impossible to tell which ground the jury selected. . . .

We conclude, therefore, that since the Communist Party came into being in 1945, and the indictment was not returned until 1951, the three-year statute of limitations had run on the "organizing" charge, and required the withdrawal of that part of the indictment from the jury's consideration. . . .

We are thus faced with the question whether the Smith Act prohibits advocacy and teaching of forcible overthrow as an abstract principle, divorced from any effort to instigate action to that end, so long as such advocacy or teaching is engaged in with evil intent. We hold that it does not. . . .

. . . The legislative history of the Smith Act and related bills shows beyond all question that Congress was aware of the distinction between the advocacy or teaching of abstract doctrine and the advocacy or teaching of action, and that it did not intend to disregard it. The statute was aimed at the advocacy and teaching of concrete action for the forcible overthrow of the Government, and not of principles divorced from action.

The Government's reliance on this Court's decision in *Dennis* is misplaced. The jury instructions which were refused here were given there, and were referred to by this Court as requiring "the jury to find the facts *essential* to establish the substantive crime." (emphasis added.) It is true that at one point in the late Chief Justice's opinion it is stated that the Smith Act "is directed at advocacy, not discussion," . . . but it is clear that the reference was to advocacy of action, not ideas, for in the very next sentence the opinion emphasizes that the jury was properly instructed that there could be no conviction for "advocacy in the realm of ideas." The two concurring opinions in that case likewise emphasize the distinction with which we are concerned. . . .

In failing to distinguish between advocacy of forcible overthrow as an abstract doctrine and advocacy of action to that end, the District Court appears to have been led astray by the holding in *Dennis* that advocacy of violent action to be

taken at some future time was enough. It seems to have considered that, since "inciting" speech is usually thought of as something calculated to induce immediate action, and since *Dennis* held advocacy of action for future overthrow sufficient, this meant that advocacy, irrespective of its tendency to generate action, is punishable, provided only that it is uttered with a specific intent to accomplish overthrow. In other words, the District Court apparently thought that *Dennis* obliterated the traditional dividing line between advocacy of abstract doctrine and advocacy of action.

This misconceives the situation confronting the Court in *Dennis* and what was held there. Although the jury's verdict, interpreted in light of the trial court's instructions, did not justify the conclusion that the defendants' advocacy was directed at, or created any danger of, immediate overthrow, it did establish that the advocacy was aimed at building up a seditious group and maintaining it in readiness for action at a propitious time. In such circumstances, said Chief Justice Vinson, the Government need not hold its hand "until the *putsch* is about to be executed, the plans have been laid and the signal is awaited. If Government is aware that a group aiming at its overthrow is attempting to indoctrinate its members and to commit them to a course whereby they will strike when the leaders feel the circumstances permit, action by the Government is required." . . . The essence of the *Dennis* holding was that indoctrination of a group in preparation for future violent action, as well as exhortation to immediate action, by advocacy found to be directed to "action for the accomplishment" of forcible overthrow, to violence as "a rule or principle of action," and employing "language of incitement," . . . is not constitutionally protected when the group is of sufficient size and cohesiveness, is sufficiently oriented towards action, and other circumstances are such as reasonably to justify apprehension that action will occur. This is quite a different thing from the view of the District Court here that mere doctrinal justification of forcible overthrow, if engaged in with the intent to accomplish overthrow, is punishable *per se* under the Smith Act. That sort of advocacy, even though uttered with the hope that it may ultimately lead to violent revolution, is too remote from concrete action to be regarded as the kind of indoctrination preparatory to action which was condemned in *Dennis*. As one of the concurring opinions in *Dennis* put it: "Throughout our decisions there has recurred a distinction between the statement of an idea which may prompt its hearers to take unlawful action, and advocacy that such action be taken." . . .

There is nothing in *Dennis* which makes that historic distinction obsolete. . . .

We recognize that distinctions between advocacy or teaching of abstract doctrines, with evil intent, and that which is directed to stirring people to action, are often subtle and difficult to grasp, for in a broad sense, as Mr. Justice Holmes said . . .: "Every idea is an incitement." But the very subtlety of these distinctions required the most clear and explicit instructions with reference to them, for they concerned an issue which went to the very heart of the charges against these petitioners. . . . Particularly in light of this record, we must regard the trial court's charge in this respect as furnishing wholly inadequate guidance to the jury on this central point in the case. We cannot allow a conviction to stand on such "an equivocal direction to the jury on a basic issue." . . .

MR. JUSTICE BLACK, *with whom* MR. JUSTICE DOUGLAS *joins, concurring in part and dissenting in part.*

I would reverse every one of these convictions and direct that all the defendants be acquitted. In my judgment the statutory provisions on which these prosecutions are based abridge freedom of speech, press and assembly in violation of the First Amendment to the United States Constitution. . . .

I . . . agree with the Court insofar as it holds that the trial judge erred in instructing that persons could be punished under the Smith Act for teaching and advocating forceful overthrow as an abstract principle. But on the other hand, I cannot agree that the instruction which the Court indicates it might approve is constitutionally permissible. The Court

says that persons can be punished for advocating action to overthrow the Government by force and violence, where those to whom the advocacy is addressed are urged "to *do* something, now or in the future, rather than merely to *believe* in something." Under the Court's approach, defendants could still be convicted simply for agreeing to talk as distinguished from agreeing to act. I believe that the First Amendment forbids Congress to punish people for talking about public affairs, whether or not such discussion incites to action, legal or illegal. . . . As the Virginia Assembly said in 1785, in its "Statute for Religious Liberty," written by Thomas Jefferson, "it is time enough for the rightful purposes of civil government, for its officers to interfere when principles break out into overt acts against peace and good order. . . ."

In essence, petitioners were tried upon the charge that they believe in and want to foist upon this country a different and to us a despicable form of authoritarian government in which voices criticizing the existing order are summarily silenced. I fear that the present type of prosecutions are more in line with the philosophy of authoritarian government than with that expressed by our First Amendment.

Doubtlessly, dictators have to stamp out causes and beliefs which they deem subversive to their evil regimes. But governmental suppression of causes and beliefs seems to me to be the very antithesis of what our Constitution stands for. The choice expressed in the First Amendment in favor of free expression was made against a turbulent background by men such as Jefferson, Madison, and Mason— men who believed that loyalty to the provisions of this Amendment was the best way to assure a long life for this new nation and its Government. Unless there is complete freedom for expression of all ideas, whether we like them or not, concerning the way government should be run and who shall run it, I doubt if any views in the long run can be secured against the censor. The First Amendment provides the only kind of security system that can preserve a free government—one that leaves the way wide open for people to favor, discuss, advocate, or incite causes and doctrines however obnoxious and antagonistic such views may be to the rest of us.

MR. JUSTICE CLARK *dissented.*

Scales v. United States

MR. JUSTICE HARLAN *delivered the opinion of the Court.*

THE Smith Act . . . among other things, makes a felony the acquisition or holding of knowing membership in any organization which advocates the overthrow of the Government of the United States by force or violence. The indictment charged that from January 1946 to the date of its filing (November 18, 1954) the Communist Party of the United States was such an organization, and that petitioner throughout that period was a member thereof, with knowledge of the Party's illegal purpose and a specific intent to accomplish overthrow "as speedily as circumstances would permit. . . ."

It will bring the constitutional issues into clear focus to notice first the premises on which the case was submitted to the jury. The jury was instructed that in order to convict it must find that within the three-year limitation period (1) the Communist Party advocated the violent overthrow of the Government, in the sense of present "advocacy of action" to

367 U.S. 203 (1961).

accomplish that end as soon as circumstances were propitious; and (2) petitioner was an "active" member of the party, and not merely "a nominal, passive, inactive or purely technical" member, with knowledge of the Party's illegal advocacy and a specific intent to bring about violent overthrow "as speedily as circumstances would permit."

The constitutional attack upon the membership clause, as thus construed, is that the statute offends (1) the Fifth Amendment, in that it impermissibly imputes guilt to an individual merely on the basis of his associations and sympathies, rather than because of some concrete personal involvement in criminal conduct; and (2) the First Amendment, in that it infringes free political expression and association. . . .

FIFTH AMENDMENT

In our jurisprudence guilt is personal, and when the imposition of punishment on a status or on conduct can only be justified by reference to the relationship of that status or conduct to other concededly criminal activity (here advocacy of violent overthrow), that relationship must be sufficiently substantial to satisfy the concept of personal guilt in order to withstand attack under the Due Process Clause of the Fifth Amendment. Membership, without more, in an organization engaged in illegal advocacy, it is now said, has not heretofore been recognized by this Court to be such a relationship. This claim stands, and we shall examine it, independently of that made under the First Amendment.

Any thought that due process puts beyond the reach of the criminal law all individual associational relationships, unless accompanied by the commission of specific acts of criminality, is dispelled by familiar concepts of the law of conspiracy and complicity. While both are commonplace in the landscape of the criminal law, they are not natural features. Rather they are particular legal concepts manifesting the more general principle that society, having the power to punish dangerous behavior, cannot be powerless against those who work to bring about that behavior. The fact that Congress has not resorted to either of these familiar concepts means only that the enquiry here must direct itself to an analysis of the relationship between the fact of membership and the underlying substantive illegal conduct, in order to determine whether that relationship is indeed too tenuous to permit its use as the basis of criminal liability. In this instance it is an organization which engages in criminal activity, and we can perceive no reason why one who actively and knowingly works in the ranks of that organization, intending to contribute to the success of those specifically illegal activities, should be any more immune from prosecution than he to whom the organization has assigned the task of carrying out the substantive criminal act. Nor should the fact that Congress has focussed here on "membership," the characteristic relationship between an individual and the type of conspiratorial quasi-political associations with the criminal aspect of whose activities Congress was concerned, of itself require the conclusion that the legislature has traveled outside the familiar and permissible bounds of criminal imputability. In truth, the specificity of the proscribed relationship is not necessarily a vice; it provides instruction and warning.

What must be met, then, is the argument that membership, even when accompanied by the elements of knowledge and specific intent, affords an insufficient quantum of participation in the organization's alleged criminal activity, that is, an insufficiently significant form of aid and encouragement to permit the imposition of criminal sanctions on that basis. It must indeed be recognized that a person who merely becomes a member of an illegal organization by that "act" alone need be doing nothing more than signifying his assent to its purposes and activities on one hand, and providing, on the other, only the sort of moral encouragement, which comes from the knowledge that others believe in what the organization is doing. It may indeed be argued that such assent and encouragement do fall short of the concrete, practical impetus given to a criminal enterprise which is lent for instance by a commitment on the part of a conspirator to act in furtherance of that enterprise. A member, as distinguished from a conspirator, may indicate his approval of a criminal enterprise by the very fact of his membership without thereby necessarily committing himself to further it by any act or course of conduct whatever. . . .

. . . These factors have weight and must be found to be overborne in a total constitutional assessment of the statute. We think, however, they are duly met when the statute is found to reach only "active" members having also a guilty knowledge and intent, and which therefore prevents a conviction on what otherwise might be regarded as merely an expression of sympathy with the alleged criminal enterprise, unaccompanied by any significant action in its support or any commitment to undertake such action.

Thus, given the construction of the membership clause already discussed, we think the factors called for in rendering members criminally responsible for the illegal advocacy of the organization fall within established, and therefore presumably constitutional standards of criminal imputability.

FIRST AMENDMENT

Little remains to be said concerning the claim that the statute infringes First Amendment freedoms. It was settled in *Dennis* that the advocacy with which we are here concerned is not constitutionally protected speech, and it was further established that a combination to promote such advocacy, albeit under the aegis of what purports to be a political party, is not such association as is protected by the First Amendment. We can discern no reason why membership, when it constitutes a purposeful form of complicity in a group engaging in this same forbidden advocacy, should receive any greater degree of protection from the guarantees of that Amendment.

If it is said that the mere existence of such an enactment tends to inhibit the exercise of constitutionally protected rights, in that it engenders an unhealthy fear that one may find himself unwittingly embroiled in criminal liability, the answer surely is that the statute provides that a defendant must be proven to have knowledge of the proscribed advocacy before he may be convicted. It is, of course, true that quasi-political parties or other groups that may embrace both legal and illegal aims differ from a technical conspiracy, which is defined by its criminal purpose, so that *all* knowing association with the conspiracy is a proper subject for criminal proscription so far as First Amendment liberties are concerned. If there were a similar blanket prohibition of association with a group having both legal and illegal aims, there would indeed be a real danger that legitimate political expression or association would be impaired, but the membership clause, as here construed, does not cut deeper into the freedom of association than is necessary to deal with "the substantive evils that Congress has a right to prevent." . . . The clause does not make criminal all association with an organization, which has been shown to engage in illegal advocacy. There must be clear proof that a defendant "specifically intend[s] to accomplish [the aims of the organization] by resort to violence." . . . Thus the member for whom the organization is a vehicle for the advancement of legitimate aims and policies does not fall within the ban of the statute: he lacks the requisite specific intent "to bring about the overthrow of the government as speedily as circumstances would permit." Such a person may be foolish, deluded, or perhaps merely optimistic, but he is not by this statute made a criminal.

We conclude that petitioner's constitutional challenge must be overruled. . . .

The judgment of the Court of Appeals must be

Affirmed.

MR. JUSTICE BLACK, *dissenting.*

I think it is important to point out the manner in which this case re-emphasizes the freedom-destroying nature of the "balancing test" presently in use by the Court to justify its refusal to apply specific constitutional protections of the Bill of Rights. In some of the recent cases in which it has "balanced" away the protections of the First Amendment, the Court has suggested that it was justified in the application of this "test" because no direct abridgment of First Amendment freedoms was involved, the abridgment in each of these cases being, in the Court's opinion, nothing more than "an incident of the informed exercise of a valid governmental function." A possible implication of that suggestion was that if the Court was confronted with what it would call a direct abridgment of speech, it would not apply the "balancing test" but would enforce the protections of the First Amendment according to its own terms. This case causes me to doubt that such an implication is justified. Petitioner is being sent to jail for the express reason that he has associated with people who have entertained unlawful ideas and said unlawful things, and that of course is a *direct* abridgment of his freedoms of speech and assembly—under any definition that has ever been used for that term. Nevertheless, even as to this admittedly direct abridgment, the Court relies upon its prior decisions to the effect that the Government has power to abridge speech and assembly if its interest in doing so is sufficient to outweigh the interest in protecting these First Amendment freedoms.

This, I think, demonstrates the unlimited breadth and danger of the "balancing test" as it is currently being applied by a majority of this Court. Under that "test," the question in every case in which a First Amendment right is asserted is not whether there has been an abridgment of that right, not whether the abridgment of that right was intentional on the part of the Government, and not whether there is any other way in which the Government could accomplish a lawful aim without an invasion of the constitutionally guaranteed rights of the people. It is, rather, simply whether the Government has an interest in abridging the right involved and, if so, whether that interest is of sufficient importance in the opinion of a majority of this Court, to justify the Government's action in doing so. This doctrine, to say the very least, is capable of being used to justify almost any action Government may wish to take to suppress First Amendment freedoms.

MR. JUSTICE DOUGLAS, *dissenting.*

When we allow petitioner to be sentenced to prison for six years for being a "member" of the Communist Party, we make a sharp break with traditional concepts of First Amendment rights and make serious Mark Twain's lighthearted comment that "it is by the goodness of God that in our country we have those three unspeakably precious things: freedom of speech, freedom of conscience, and the prudence never to practice either of them." . . .

There is here no charge of conspiracy, no charge of any overt act to overthrow the Government by force and violence, no charge of any other criminal act. The charge is being a "member" of the Communist Party, "well-knowing" that it advocated the overthrow of the Government by force and violence, "said defendant intending to bring about such overthrow by force and violence, as speedily as circumstances would permit." That falls far short of a charge of conspiracy. Conspiracy rests not in intention alone but in an agreement with one or more others to promote an unlawful project. . . . No charge of any kind or sort of agreement hitherto embraced in the concept of a conspiracy is made here.

We legalize today guilt by association, sending a man to prison when he committed no unlawful act. . . .

The case is not saved by showing that petitioner was an active member. None of the activity constitutes a crime. The record contains evidence that Scales was the Chairman of the North and South Carolina Districts of the Communist Party. He recruited new members into the Party, and promoted the advanced education of selected young Party members in the theory of communism to be undertaken at secret schools. He was a director of one such school. He explained the principles of the Party to an FBI agent who posed as someone interested in joining the Party, and furnished him literature, including articles which criticized in vivid language the American "aggression" in Korea and described American "atrocities" committed on Korean citizens. He once remarked that the Party was setting up underground means of communication, and in 1951 he himself "went underground." At the school of which Scales was director, students were told (by someone else) that one of the Party's weaknesses was in failing to place people in key industrial positions. One witness told of a meeting arranged by Scales at which the staff of the school urged him to remain in his position in an industrial plant rather than return to college. In Scales' presence, students at the school were once shown how to kill a person with a pencil, a device which, it was said, might come in handy on a picket line. Other evidence showed Scales to have made several statements or distributed literature containing implicating passages. Among them were comments to the effect that the Party line was that the Negroes in the South and the working classes should be used to foment a violent revolution; that a

Communist government could not be voted into power in this country because the Government controlled communication media, newspapers, the military, and the educational systems, and that force was the only way to achieve the revolution; that if a depression were to come the Communist America would be closer at hand than predicted by William Z. Foster; that the revolution would come within a generation; that it would be easier in the United States than in Russia to effectuate the revolution because of assistance and advice from Russian Communists. Petitioner at different times said or distributed literature which said that the goals of communism could only be achieved by violent revolution that would have to start internally with the working classes.

Not one single illegal act is charged to petitioner. That is why the essence of the crime covered by the indictment is merely belief—belief in the proletarian revolution, belief in Communist creed. . . .

Nothing but beliefs are on trial in this case. They are unpopular and to most of us revolting. But they are nonetheless ideas or dogma or faith within the broad framework of the First Amendment. . . .

Belief in the principle of revolution is deep in our traditions. The Declaration of Independence proclaims it:

Whenever any Form of Government becomes destructive of these ends, it is the Right of the People to alter or abolish it, and to institute new Government, laying its foundation on such principles and organizing its powers in such form, as to them shall seem most likely to effect their Safety and Happiness.

This right of revolution has been and is a part of the fabric of our institutions. . . .

Of course, government can move against those who take up arms against it. Of course, the constituted authority has the right of self-preservation. But we deal in this prosecution of Scales only with the legality of ideas and beliefs, not with overt acts. The Court speaks of the prevention of "dangerous behavior" by punishing those "who work to bring about that behavior." That formula returns man to the dark days when government determined what behavior was "dangerous" and then policed the dissidents for tell-tale signs of advocacy. . . .

MR. JUSTICE BRENNAN *with whom* THE CHIEF JUSTICE *and* MR. JUSTICE DOUGLAS *join, dissenting.*

I think that in sec. 4(f) of the Internal Security Act Congress legislated immunity from prosecution under the membership clause of the Smith Act. The first sentence of sec. 4(f) is: "Neither the holding of office nor membership in any Communist organization by any person shall constitute per se a violation of subsection (a) or subsection (c) of this section or of any other criminal statute." The immunity granted by that sentence is not in my view restricted, as the Court holds, to *mere* membership, that is to membership which is nominal, passive or theoretical. The immunity also extends to "active and purposive membership, purposive that is as to the organization's criminal ends," which is the character of membership to which the Court today restricts the application of the membership clause of the Smith Act. . . .

Noto v. United States

MR. JUSTICE HARLAN *delivered the opinion of the Court.*

THIS case, like *Scales v. United States,* . . . was brought here to test the validity of a conviction under the membership clause of the Smith Act. . . .

The only one of petitioner's points we need consider is his attack on the sufficiency of the evidence, since his statutory and constitutional challenges to the conviction are disposed of by our opinion in *Scales;* and consideration of his other contentions is rendered unnecessary by the view we take of his evidentiary challenge.

In considering that challenge we start from the premise that Smith Act offenses require rigorous standards of proof. . . . We find that the record in this case . . . requires us to conclude that the evidence of illegal Party advocacy was insufficient to support this conviction.

A large part of the evidence adduced by the Government on that issue came from the witness Lautner, and the reading of copious excerpts from the "communist classics." This evidence, to be sure, plentifully shows the Party's teaching of abstract doctrine that revolution is an inevitable product of the "proletarian" effort to achieve communism in a capitalist society, but testimony as to happenings which might have lent that evidence to an inference of "advocacy of action" to accomplish that end during the period of the indictment, 1946-1954, or itself supported such an inference, is sparse indeed. Moreover, such testimony as there is of that nature was not broadly based, but was limited almost exclusively to Party doings in western New York, more especially in the cities of Rochester

and Buffalo, the scene of petitioner's principal Party activities. Further, the showing of illegal Party advocacy lacked the compelling quality which in *Scales* . . . was supplied by the petitioner's own utterances and systematic course of conduct as a high Party official. We proceed to a summary of this testimony.

The witness Dietch described mainly episodes from his indoctrination as a member of the Rochester Young Communist League during the years 1935-1938 . . . , and testified that petitioner, then a youth, was an active and convinced member of the League. . . . Dietch's testimony referred to one possibly relevant episode, when, in 1951, he obtained for the Party at petitioner's request two pieces of special printing equipment for which petitioner paid $100 and $200. However, this episode is deprived of significance when it appears from the witness' testimony that petitioner explained to him at the time that pressure brought to bear on the Party had made it difficult for it to get its printing done by conventional commercial means.

The witness Geraldine Hicks had joined the Party in 1943 at the request of the F.B.I. . . . Her testimony related to classes and meetings which she attended in the Buffalo area, where the "communist classics" were used for teaching purposes. Extensive passages from these works were read into evidence. She also testified as to the importance attributed by the local Party to its "industrial concentration" work and to its recruitment of workers in those industries as well as to the importance attributed to the recruitment of Negroes.

The witness Chatley, who was a bus driver during the period of his Communist Party membership . . . testified to Party teachings as to the importance of receiving solid support from the labor unions. . . . Perhaps the most significant item of Chatley's testimony dealt with an interview with petitioner, at which Chatley was requested to hide out a Party member who was fleeing the F.B.I. in connection with "what the newspapers called this Atom Spy Ring business." So far as the record reveals, the plans never progressed beyond this request. The petitioner had also told Chatley that the Federal Government was building concentration camps. . . .

Certainly the most damaging testimony came from the witness Regan, who as a government agent and Party member . . . gathered considerable information on the Party's "industrial concentration" program. . . . Regan also received a pamphlet, but not from the petitioner, . . . [which] stated at one point:

1. Three basic industries, steel, railroad, and mining. These are basis [sic] to the National economy, that is if any one or all three are shut down by strike our economy is paralyzed. It is necessary for a Marxist revolutionary party to be rooted in these industries. . . .

. . . Speaking of the war in Korea, Regan testified that the petitioner had said at the conference of the Upstate District of the Party in 1950:

". . . the war . . . was caused by an aggressive action of the United States, American troops would follow Wall Street policy. He said it is possible for this to break out in other parts of the world. He mentioned the near East.

"Q. Is that all?

"A. Yes."

No effort was made to link up this conference with particularly trusted Party members. . . .

[Regan] recalled [an] intemperate remark by the petitioner during a meeting in 1947:

Lumpkin [a Party member] was talking about a visit to his home by a local newspaper reporter. He said the reporter came to his home. They let him in and answered a lot of questions. . . .

John Noto said Lumpkin should never let the reporter into the house. Should not have answered any questions. He said "Sometime I will see the time we can stand a person like this S.O.B. against the wall and shoot him."

The witness Greenberg testified largely about the Party program . . . as to setting up printing and mimeographing equipment in case commercial channels were cut off or the Party was forced underground. . . .

Finally, there was testimony through the witness Lautner as to the Party's underground organization . . . including petitioner's participation therein as one of the three Party members in charge.

We must consider this evidence in the light most favorable to the Government to see whether it would support the conclusion that the Party engaged in the advocacy "not of . . . mere abstract doctrine of forcible overthrow, but of action to that end, by the use of language reasonably and ordinarily calculated to incite persons to . . . action" immediately or in the future. [In] *Yates* v. *United States*, . . . we said:

. . . The essence of the *Dennis* holding was that indoctrination of a group in preparation for future violent action, as well as exhortation to immediate action, by advocacy found to be directed to "action for the accomplishment" of forcible overthrow, to violence as "a rule or principle of action," and employing "language of incitement" . . . is not constitutionally protected. . . . This is quite a different thing from the view of the District Court here that mere doctrinal justification of forcible overthrow, if engaged in with intent to accomplish overthrow, is punishable *per se* under the Smith Act. That sort of advocacy, even though uttered with the hope that it may ultimately lead to violent revolution, is too remote from concrete action to be regarded as the kind of indoctrination preparatory to action which was condemned in *Dennis*. As one of the concurring opinions in *Dennis* put it: "Throughout our decisions there has recurred a distinction between the statement of an idea which may prompt its hearers to take unlawful action, and advocacy that such action be taken." . . .

. . . We reiterate now, that the mere abstract teaching of Communist theory, including the teaching of the moral propriety or even moral necessity for a resort to force and violence, is not the same as preparing a group for violent action and steeling it to such action. There must be some substantial direct or circumstantial evidence of a call to violence now or in the future which is both sufficiently strong and sufficiently pervasive to lend color to the otherwise ambiguous theoretical material regarding Communist Party teaching, and to justify the inference that such a call to violence may fairly be imputed to the Party as a whole, and not merely to some narrow segment of it.

Surely the offhand remarks that certain individuals hostile to the Party would one day be shot cannot demonstrate more than the venomous or spiteful attitude of the Party towards its enemies, and might indicate what could be expected from the Party if it should ever succeed to power. The "industrial concentration" program, as to which the witness Regan testified in some detail, does

indeed come closer to the kind of concrete and particular program on which a criminal conviction in this sort of case must be based. But in examining that evidence it appears to us that, in the context of this record, this too fails to establish that the Communist Party was an organization which presently advocated violent overthrow of the Government now or in the future, for that is what must be proven. The most that can be said is that the evidence as to that program might justify an inference that the leadership of the Party was preparing the way for a situation in which future acts of sabotage might be facilitated, but there is no evidence that such acts of sabotage were presently advocated; and it is *present* advocacy, and not an intent to advocate in the future or a conspiracy to advocate in the future once a groundwork has been laid, which is an element of the crime under the membership clause. To permit an inference of present advocacy from evidence showing at best only a purpose or conspiracy to advocate in the future would be to allow the jury to blur the lines of distinction between the various offenses punishable under the Smith Act.

The kind of evidence which we found in *Scales* sufficient to support the jury's verdict of present illegal Party advocacy is lacking here in any adequately substantial degree. It need hardly be said that it is upon the particular evidence in a particular record that a particular defendant must be judged, and not upon the evidence in some other record or upon what may be supposed to be the tenets of the Communist Party. . . .

In view of our conclusion as to the insufficiency of the evidence as to illegal Party advocacy, the judgment of the Court of Appeals must be

Reversed.

MR. JUSTICE BLACK, *concurring*.

In 1799, the English Parliament passed a law outlawing certain named societies on the ground that they were engaged in "a traitorous Conspiracy . . . in conjunction with the Persons from Time to Time exercising the Powers of Government in *France*. . . ." One of the many strong arguments made by those who opposed the enactment of this law was stated by a member of that body, Mr. Tierney:

The remedy proposed goes to the putting an end to all these societies together. I object to the system, of which this is only a branch; for the right hon. gentleman has told us he intends to propose laws from time to time upon this subject, as cases may arise to require them. I say these attempts lead to consequences of the most horrible kind. . . . Those whom [he] cannot prove to be guilty, [he] will punish for their suspicion. To support this system, we must have a swarm of spies and informers. They are the very pillars of such a system of government.

The decision in this case, in my judgment, dramatically illustrates the continuing vitality of this observation.

The conviction of the petitioner here is being reversed because the Government has failed to produce evidence the Court believes sufficient to prove that the Communist Party presently advocates the overthrow of the Government by force. The Government is being told, in effect, that if it wishes to get convic-tions under the Smith Act, it must maintain a permanent staff of informers who are prepared to give up-to-date information with respect to the present policies of the Communist Party. Given the fact that such prosecutions are to be permitted at all, I do not disagree with the wisdom of the Court's decision to compel the Government to come forward with evidence to prove its charges in each particular case. But I think that it is also important to realize the overriding pre-eminence that such a system of laws gives to the perpetuation and encouragement of the practice of informing—a practice which, I think it is fair to say, has not always been considered the sort of system to which a wise government would entrust the security of a Nation. I have always thought, as I still do think, that this Government was built upon a foundation strong enough to assure its endurance without resort to practices which most of us think of as being associated only with totalitarian governments.

I cannot join an opinion which implies that the existence of liberty is dependent upon the efficiency of the Government's informers. I prefer to rest my concurrence in the judgment reversing petitioner's conviction on what I regard as the more solid ground that the First Amendment forbids the Government to abridge the rights of freedom of speech, press and assembly.

THE McCARRAN ACT

To protect the United States against certain un-American and subversive activities by requiring registration of Communist organizations, and for other purposes. . . .

SEC. 1. (b) Nothing in this Act shall be construed to authorize, require or establish military or civilian censorship or in any way to limit or infringe upon freedom of the press or of speech as guaranteed by the Constitution of the United States and no regulation shall be promulgated hereunder having that effect.

NECESSITY FOR LEGISLATION

SEC. 2. As a result of evidence adduced before various committees of the Senate and House of Representatives, the Congress hereby finds that—

(1) There exists a world Communist movement which, in its origins, its development, and its present practice, is a world-wide revolutionary movement whose purpose it is, by treachery, deceit, infiltration into other groups (governmental and otherwise), espionage, sabotage, terrorism, and any other means deemed necessary, to establish a Communist totalitarian dictatorship in the countries throughout the world through the medium of a world-wide Communist organization. . . .

(4) The direction and control of the world Communist movement is vested in and exercised by the Communist dictatorship of a foreign country.

(5) The Communist dictatorship of such foreign country, in exercising such direction and control and in furthering the purposes of the world Communist movement, establishes or causes the establishment of, and utilizes, in various countries, action organizations which are not free and independent organizations, but are sections of a world-wide Communist organization and are controlled, directed, and subject to the discipline of the Communist dictatorship of such foreign country. . . .

(11) The agents of communism have devised clever and ruthless espionage and sabotage tactics which are carried out in many instances in form or manner successfully evasive of existing law. . . .

(15) The Communist movement in the United States is an organization numbering thousands of adherents, rigidly and ruthlessly disciplined. Awaiting and seeking to advance a moment when the United States may be so far extended by foreign engagements, so far divided in counsel, or so far in industrial or financial straits, that overthrow of the Government of the United States by force and violence may seem possible of achievement, it seeks converts far and wide by an extensive system of schooling and indoctrination. Such preparations by Communist organizations in other countries have aided in supplanting existing governments. The Communist organization in the United States, pursuing its stated objectives, the recent successes of Communist methods in other countries, and the nature and control of the world Communist movement itself, present a clear and present danger to the security of the United States and to the existence of free American institutions, and make it necessary that Congress, in order to provide for the common defense, to preserve the sovereignty of the United States as an independent nation, and to guarantee to each State a republi-

Public Law 831—81st Congress.

can form of government, enact appropriate legislation recognizing the existence of such world-wide conspiracy and designed to prevent it from accomplishing its purpose in the United States.

REGISTRATION . . . OF COMMUNIST ORGANIZATIONS

SEC. 7. (a) Each Communist-action organization (including any organization required, by a final order of the Board, to register as a Communist-action organization) shall, within the time specified in subsection (c) of this section, register with the Attorney General, on a form prescribed by him by regulations, as a Communist-action organization.

(b) Each Communist-front organization (including any organization required, by a final order of the Board, to register as a Communist-front organization) shall, within the time specified in subsection (c) of this section, register with the Attorney General, on a form prescribed by him by regulations, as a Communist-front organization. . . .

REGISTRATION OF MEMBERS OF COMMUNIST-ACTION ORGANIZATIONS

SEC. 8. (a) Any individual who is or becomes a member of any organization concerning which (1) there is in effect a final order of the Board requiring such organization to register under section 7 (a) of this title as a Communist-action organization, (2) more than thirty days have elapsed since such order has become final, and (3) such organization is not registered under section 7 of this title as a Communist-action organization, shall within sixty days after said order has become final, or within thirty days after becoming a member of such organization, whichever is later, register with the Attorney General as a member of such organization. . . .

COMMUNIST CONTROL ACT OF 1954

SEC. 2. The Congress hereby finds and declares that the Communist Party of the United States, although purportedly a political party, is in fact an instrumentality of a conspiracy to overthrow the Government of the United States. It constitutes an authoritarian dictatorship within a republic, demanding for itself the rights and privileges accorded to political parties, but denying to all others the liberties guaranteed by the Constitution. Unlike political parties, which evolve their policies and programs through public means, by the reconciliation of a wide variety of individual views, and submit those policies and programs to the electorate at large for approval or disapproval, the policies and programs of the Communist Party are secretly prescribed for it by the foreign leaders of the world Communist movement. Its members have no part in determining its goals, and are not permitted to voice dissent to party objectives. Unlike members of political parties, members of the Communist Party are recruited for indoctrination with respect to its objectives and methods, and are organized, instructed, and disciplined to carry into action slavishly the assignments given them by their hierarchical chieftains. Unlike political parties, the Communist Party acknowledges no constitutional or statutory limitations upon its conduct or upon that of its members. The Communist Party is relatively small

Public Law 637—83rd Congress.

numerically, and gives scant indication of capacity ever to attain its ends by lawful political means. The peril inherent in its operation arises not from its numbers, but from its failure to acknowledge any limitation as to the nature of its activities, and its dedication to the proposition that the present constitutional Government of the United States ultimately must be brought to ruin by any available means, including resort to force and violence. Holding that doctrine, its role as the agency of a hostile foreign power renders its existence a clear present and continuing danger to the security of the United States. It is the means whereby individuals are seduced into the service of the world Communist movement, trained to do its bidding, and directed and controlled in the conspiratorial performance of their revolutionary services. Therefore, the Communist Party should be outlawed.

SEC. 3. The Communist Party of the United States, or any successors of such party regardless of the assumed name, whose object or purpose is to overthrow the Government of the United States, or the government of any State, Territory, District, or possession thereof, or the government of any political subdivision therein by force and violence, are not entitled to any of the rights, privileges, and immunities attendant upon legal bodies created under the jurisdiction of the laws of the United States or any political subdivision thereof; and whatever rights, privileges, and immunities which have heretofore been granted to said party or any subsidiary organization by reason of the laws of the United States or any political subdivision thereof, are hereby terminated: *Provided, however, That* nothing in this section shall be construed as amending the Internal Security Act of 1950, as amended.

Communist Party v. Subversive Activities Control Board

MR. JUSTICE FRANKFURTER *delivered the opinion of the Court.*

THIS is a proceeding pursuant to sec. 14(a) of the Subversive Activities Control Act of 1950 to review an order of the Subversive Activities Control Board requiring the Communist Party of the United States to register as a Communist-action organization under sec. 7 of the Act. The Court of Appeals for the District of Columbia has affirmed the Board's registration order. Because important questions of construction and constitutionality of the statute were raised by the Party's petition for certiorari, we brought the case here. . . .

This litigation has a long history. On

November 22, 1950, the Attorney General petitioned the Subversive Activities Control Board for an order to require that the Communist Party register as a Communist-action organization. . . .

We come [now] to the Communist Party's contentions that the Board and the Court of Appeals erred in their construction of the Act and in their application of it, on the facts of this record, to the Party. . . .

A. *The "Control Component."* Under sec. 3(3) of the Act an organization cannot be found to be a Communist-action organization unless it is "substantially

367 U.S. 1 (1961).

directed, dominated, or controlled by the foreign government or foreign organization controlling the world Communist movement. . . ." The Party asserts that this requirement is not satisfied by any lesser demonstration than that the foreign government or foreign organization controlling the world Communist movement exercises over the organization an enforceable, coercive power to exact compliance with its demands. The Court of Appeals disagreed, holding that in the circumstances of this record a consistent, undeviating dedication, over an extended period of time, to carrying out the programs of the foreign government or foreign organization, despite significant variations in direction of those programs, was sufficient. . . .

. . . We cannot hold that they [The Board and The Court below] erred in the construction of the statute and in finding that the facts shown bring the Party within it.

B. *The "Objectives Component."* Section 3(3), defining a Communist-action organization, requires a finding that the organization "operates primarily to advance the objectives of [the] . . . world Communist movement as referred to in section 2 of this title." Although asserting that the reference to sec. 2 is unclear, the Party offered in the Court of Appeals a construction of this requirement which defines the objectives of the world Communist movement as (a) overthrow of existing government by any means necessary, including force and violence, (b) establishment of a Communist totalitarian dictatorship, (c) which will be subservient to the Soviet Union. . . . The Court of Appeals accepted the Party's analysis *arguendo,* and its judgment affirming the order of the Board rests on its conclusion that the Party operates to advance all three of these

objectives. This conclusion is supported by the findings of the Board. It adopts the interpretation most favorable to the Party.

Within the framework of these definitions, the Court of Appeals held sufficient to demonstrate the Communist Party's objective to overthrow existing government the finding of the Board that the Party advocates the overthrow of the Government of the United States by force and violence if necessary. The Party argues that this finding is inadequate. . . . We think that an organization may be found to operate to advance objectives [of Sec. 2 of the Act] although it does not incite the present use of force. Nor does the First Amendment compel any other construction. The Subversive Activities Control Act is a regulatory, not a prohibitory statute. It does not make unlawful pursuit of the objectives which section 2 defines. . . .

D. *The Board Findings as to the World Communist Movement; Evidence of Past Practices; the Preponderance of the Evidence.* . . . In the present proceeding, the Board, after recognizing that "in section 2 of the Act Congress has found the existence of a world Communist movement and has described its characteristics," set forth its own description, based on the evidence presented in this record, of contemporary Communist institutions in their international aspect, and particularly of the role of the Soviet Union in those institutions. The Party argues that because this description does not duplicate in all details that of section 2 of the Act, the world Communist movement to which the Board found that the Communist Party bore the required statutory relationship is not the world Communist movement referred to in section 2.

But the attributes of the world Communist movement which are detailed in the legislative findings are not in the nature of a requisite category of characteristics comprising a definition of an entity whose existence *vel non* must be established, by proving those characteristics, in each administrative proceeding under the Act. Congress has itself found that that movement exists. The legislative description of its nature is not made a subject of litigation for the purpose of ascertaining the status of a particular organization under the Act. The Attorney General need not prove, in the case of each organization against whom a petition for a registration order is filed, that the international institutions to which the organization can be shown to be related fit the picture in every precise detail set forth in sec. 2. The only question, once an organization is found to have certain international relations, is one of statutory interpretation—of identifying the statutory referent. Are the institutions involved in those relations the "world Communist movement" to which Congress referred? We are satisfied from the Board's report that the "world Communist movement" to which its findings related the Communist Party was the same "world Communist movement" meant by Congress. . . .

The Party's constitutional attack on the Subversive Activities Control Act of 1950 assails virtually every provision of this extended and intricate regulatory statute. The registration requirement of sec. 7, by demanding self-subjection to what may be deemed a defamatory characterization and, in addition, disclosure of the identity of all rank-and-file members, is said to abridge the First Amendment rights of free expression and association of the Communist Party and its adherents. The Party's officers, it is asserted, who by filing a registration statement in its behalf evidence their status as active members of the Party, are required to incriminate themselves in violation of the Fifth Amendment, as are the individual members who must register themselves under sec. 8 if the Party fails to register or fails to list them. The provision that Communist organizations label their publications is attacked as a prior restraint on, and such sanctions as denial of tax exemption are attacked as a penalty on the exercise of, the Party's constitutionally protected freedom of speech. The various consequences of the Party's registration for its individual members—prohibition of application for and use of passports, disqualification from government or defense-facility employment, disqualification from naturalization, subjection to denaturalization, proscription of officership or employment in labor organizations—are said to deny those members due process of law by, in effect, attainting them by association, and by subjecting them to potential criminal proceedings in which the nature of the organization, membership in which is an element of various offenses, may not be judicially tried. Many of the statute's provisions are challenged as unconstitutionally vague, and it is said that the establishment of an agency, the Subversive Activities Control Board, whose continued existence depends upon its finding the Communist Party a Communist-action organization within the meaning of the Act, necessarily biases the agency and deprives the Party of a fair hearing. In fact, the Party asserts, the statute as written so particularly designates the Communist Party as the organization at which it is aimed that it constitutes an abolition of the Party by legislative fiat, in the nature of a bill of attainder. The provisions must be read as a whole, it is said; and when so read, they are seen to envisage not the registration and regulation of the Party, but the imposition of impossible requirements whose only purpose is to lay a foundation for criminal prosecution of the Party and its officers and members, in effect "outlawing" the Party.

Many of these questions are prematurely raised in this litigation. Merely potential impairment of constitutional rights under a statute does not of itself create a justiciable controversy in which the nature and extent of those rights may be litigated. . . .

This proceeding was brought by the Attorney General under sec. 13(a) of the Subversive Activities Control Act, seeking an order of the Board that the Communist Party register as a Communist-action organization pursuant to sec. 7. The Board has issued such an order, in accordance with sec. 13(g) (1), which is here reviewed, under sec. 14(a). The effect of that order is to require the Party to register and to file a registration statement within thirty days after the order becomes final, sec. 7(c) (3), upon pain of fine up to $10,000 for each day of failure to register. When the order becomes final, other consequences also ensue, for its members and for other persons. Certain acts of the Party—distributing its publications through the mails or through the instrumentalities of interstate or foreign commerce, or causing matter to be broadcast by radio or television, without the required identification—are prohibited, sec. 10, and tax exemption is denied, sec. 11. Specified acts of its members— e.g., applying for or using a United States passport, holding government or defense-facility employment, holding labor union office or employment—are forbidden, secs. 5, 6, and those members are definitively subject to certain disqualifications—if aliens they may not enter the United States, may be deported, may

not be naturalized, may in some circumstances be denaturalized, with qualifications. . . . Employment by the Party is not "employment" for purposes of the Social Security Act, as amended . . . contributions to the Party are not tax deductible . . . sec. 11. Acts by third parties with regard to the Party or its members—the contributing of funds or services to the Party by government or defense-facility personnel, issuance of passports to Party members—are, under specified circumstances, prohibited, secs. 5, 6. All of these consequences depend upon action taken subsequent to the time when the registration order becomes final. Some depend upon action which is, at best, highly contingent. The question is which, if any, of these consequences are now before us for constitutional adjudication, as necessarily involved in the determination of the constitutionality of the Board's registration order. . . .

[The] Act, . . . has a section directing that if any of its provisions, or any of its applications, is held invalid, the remaining provisions and other possible applications shall not be affected. The authoritative legislative history clearly demonstrates that a major purpose of the enactment was to regulate Communist-action organizations by means of the public disclosure effected by registration, apart from the other regulatory provisions of the Act. Such is, of course, the very purpose of the severability clause. This being so, our consideration of any other provisions than those of section 7, requiring Communist-action organizations to register and file a registration statement, could in no way affect our decision in the present case. Were every portion of the Act purporting to regulate or prohibit the conduct of registered organizations (or organizations ordered to register) and of their members, as such, unconstitutional, we would still have to affirm the judgment below. Expatiation on the validity of those portions would remain mere pronouncements, addressed to future and hypothetical controversies. This is true with regard to those sections of the Act which prescribe consequences legally enforceable against the Communist Party once a final registration order is in effect against it—the "labeling" and tax-exemption denial provisions of secs. 10 and 11. . . . Although they become operative as soon as a registration order is made final, their application remains in a very real sense problematical. We cannot now foresee what effect, if any, upon the Party the denial of tax exemption will have. We do not know whether the Party now has, or whether it will have at any time after a Board order goes into effect, any taxable income, or, indeed, any income whatever. We do not know that, after such an order is in effect, the Party will wish to utilize the mails or any instrumentality of interstate commerce for the circulation of its publications. We cannot guess the nature of whatever publications it may wish to circulate, or their relation to the purposes and functions of the Party. These circumstances may be critical for constitutional determination. It will not do to discount their significance by saying, now, that no difference in circumstances will effect a different constitutional result—that the principles relevant to a determination of the validity of these statutory provisions do not depend upon the variations in circumstances in which they are potentially applicable. For this analysis presupposes that we now understand what are the relevant constitutional principles, whereas the reason of postponing decision until a constitutional issue is more clearly focused by, and receives the impact from, occurrence in

particular circumstances is precisely that those circumstances may reveal relevancies that abstract, prospective supposition may not see or adequately assess.

These considerations are equally appropriate in the case of those sections of the Act which proscribe specified conduct by members of an organization concerning which a final registration order is in effect, or which impose obligations upon them, or which subject them to described disabilities under certain circumstances. It is wholly speculative now to foreshadow whether, or under what conditions, a member of the Party may in the future apply for a passport, or seek government or defense-facility or labor-union employment, or, being an alien, become a party to a naturalization or a denaturalization proceeding. None of these things may happen. If they do, appropriate administrative and judicial procedures will be available to test the constitutionality of applications of particular sections of the Act to particular persons in particular situations. Nothing justifies previsioning those issues now.

But the Party argues that the threat, however indefinite, of future application of these provisions to penalize individuals who are or become its members, affiliates or contributors, will effectively deter persons from associating with or from aiding and supporting it. Thus, the provisions exercise a present effect upon the Party sufficiently prejudicial to justify its challenging them in this proceeding. In support of this contention, the Party cites cases in which we have held that litigants had "standing" to attack a statute or regulation which operated to coerce other persons to withdraw from profitable relations or associations with the litigants. But these cases purported only to discuss what issues a litigant might raise, not when he might raise them. That a proper party is before the court is no answer to the objection that he is there prematurely. In none of the cases cited was the constitutional issue decided on a record which showed only potential deterrence of association with the litigant on the part of an unnamed and uncounted number of persons. . . .

The present proceeding differs from all of these. The record here does not show that any present members, affiliates, or contributors of the Party have withdrawn because of the threatened consequences to them of its registration under the Subversive Activities Control Act, or that any prospective members, affiliates, or contributors have been deterred from joining the Party or giving it their support. . . .

The constitutional contentions raised by the Party with respect to the registration requirement of sec. 7 are (A) that that requirement, in the context of the Act, in effect "outlaws" the Party and is in the nature of a bill of attainder; (B) that compelling organizations to register and to list their members on a showing merely that they are foreign-dominated and operate primarily to advance the objectives of the world Communist movement constitutes a restraint on freedom of expression and association in violation of the First Amendment; (C) that requiring Party officers to file registration statements for the Party subjects them to self-incrimination forbidden by the Fifth Amendment; (D) that the Act violates due process by legislative predetermination of facts essential to bring the Communist Party within the definitions of a Communist-action organization, and that the evidentiary elements prescribed for consideration by the Board bear no rational relation to that definition; (E) that in several aspects the Act is uncon-

stitutionally vague; and (F) that the Subversive Activities Control Board is so necessarily biased against the Communist Party as to deprive it of a fair hearing.

A. *"Outlawry" and Attainder.* Our determination that in the present proceeding all questions are premature which regard only the constitutionality of the various particular consequences of a registration order to a registered organization and its members, does not foreclose the Party from arguing—and it does argue—that in light of the cumulative effect of those consequences the registration provisions of sec. 7 are not what they seem, but represent a legislative attempt, by devious means, to "outlaw" the Party. The registration requirement, the Party contends, was designed not with the purpose of having Communist-action organizations register, but with a purpose to make it impossible to register, because of the onerous consequences of registration, and thus to establish a pretext for criminal prosecution of the organization and its members. The Act is said to be aimed particularly at the Communist Party as an identifiable entity, intending to punish it, and in this aspect to constitute a bill of attainder prohibited by Art. I, sec. 9, cl. 3 of the Constitution.

Of course, "only the clearest proof could suffice to establish the unconstitutionality of a statute on such a ground." . . . No such proof is offered here. The Act on its face gives no indication that the registration provisions were not intended to be complied with. None of the consequences which attach to registration, whatever may be their validity when weighed separately in the constitutional balance, is so devoid of rational relation to the purposes of the Act as expressed in its second section that it appears a mere pressuring device meant to catch an organization between two fires. Section 2 recites that the world Communist movement, whose purpose is to employ deceit, secrecy, infiltration, and sabotage as means to establish a Communist totalitarian dictatorship, establishes and utilizes action organizations. The Act requires such organizations to register and to label their communications, and prohibits their members from government, defense-facility and certain labor-organization employment. Section 2 sets forth that Communist-action organizations are sections of a worldwide Communist movement and that international travel of its members and agents facilitates the purpose of the movement. The Act restricts the ingress and access to United States citizenship of alien members of Communist-action organizations and deprives all members of the use of United States passports. Section 2 finds that Communist-action organizations purpose to overthrow the Government of the United States by any available, necessary means. The Act forbids government and defense-facility employees to support such organizations, and withdraws from the organizations and their contributors certain tax exemptions. None of this is so lacking in consonance as to suggest a clandestine purpose behind the registration provisions. Nor does the legislative history contain any such suggestion. Rather, the Committee reports on the bills from which the Act derived express an object "to require the Communist movement in the United States to operate in the open rather than underground," and "to expose the Communist movement and protect the public against innocent and unwitting collaboration with it."

It is true, as the Party asserts, that bills had been introduced in Congress that would have applied to the Communist Party by name, and it is no doubt also true that the form which the Subversive Activities Control Act finally took was dictated in part by constitutional scruples against outlawing of the Party by "legislative fiat." It is probable, too, that the legislators who voted for the Act in its final form expected that the Communist Party, if it continued to engage in the activities which had been reported to Congress as characterizing its past conduct, would be required to register under sec. 7. From this the Party would have us conclude that the Act is only an instrument serving to abolish the Communist Party by indirection. But such an analysis ignores our duty of respect for the exercise of the legislative power of Congress, and, more specifically, ignores the crucial constitutional significance of what Congress did when it rejected the approach of outlawing the Party by name and accepted instead a statutory program regulating not enumerated organizations but designated activities. We would be indulging in a revisory power over enactments as they come from Congress—a power which the Framers of the Constitution withheld from this Court—if we so interpreted what Congress refused to do and what in fact Congress did; that is, if we treated this Act as merely a ruse by Congress to evade constitutional safeguards. . . .

The Act is not a bill of attainder. It attaches not to specified organizations but to described activities in which an organization may or may not engage. The singling out of an individual for legislatively prescribed punishment constitutes an attainder whether the individual is called by name or described in terms of conduct which, because it is past conduct, operates only as a designation of particular persons. . . . The Subversive Activities Control Act is not of that kind. It requires the registration only of organizations which, after the date of the Act, are found to be under the direction, domination, or control of certain foreign powers and to operate primarily to advance certain objectives. This finding must be made after full administrative hearing, subject to judicial review which opens the record for the reviewing court's determination whether the administrative findings as to fact are supported by the preponderance of the evidence. Present activity constitutes an operative element to which the statute attaches legal consequences, not merely a point of reference for the ascertainment of particular persons ineluctably designated by the legislature.

The fact that activity engaged in prior to the enactment of the legislation may be regarded administratively and judicially as relevant to a determination that an organization is presently foreign-controlled and presently works to advance the objectives of the world Communist movement, does not alter the operative structure of the Act. The incidents which it reaches are nonetheless present incidents. The past is pertinent only as probative of these. In this proceeding the Board has found, and the Court of Appeals has sustained its conclusion, that the Communist Party, by virtue of the activities in which it now engages, comes within the terms of the Act. If the Party should at any time choose to abandon these activities, after it is once registered pursuant to sec. 7, the Act provides adequate means of relief. As often as once a year it may apply to the Attorney General for cancellation of registration, and in the event of his refusal to remove it from the register and to relieve it from the duty of filing annual statements, it may petition the Board for a redetermination of its amenability to the registra-

tion requirements of the Act, pursuant to a hearing which, again, is subject to judicial review. . . . Far from attaching to the past and ineradicable actions of an organization, the application of the registration section is made to turn upon continuing contemporaneous fact; its obligations arise only because, and endure only so long as, an organization presently conducts operations of a described character.

Nor is the statute made an act of "outlawry" or of attainder by the fact that the conduct which it regulates is described with such particularity that, in probability, few organizations will come within the statutory terms. Legislatures may act to curb behavior which they regard as harmful to the public welfare, whether that conduct is found to be engaged in by many persons or by one. So long as the incidence of legislation is such that the persons who engage in the regulated conduct, be they many or few, can escape regulation merely by altering the course of their own present activities, there can be no complaint of an attainder. It would be ingenuous to refuse to recognize that the Subversive Activities Control Act of 1950 was designed to reach the Communist Party's operations as then reported to Congress—operations in which, the Board has found, the Party persists. But to base a determination of constitutionality on this design would be to confuse the occasion of legislation with its operative effect and consequently to mistake decisive constitutional determinants. No doubt, the activity whose regulation the Act seeks to achieve is activity historically associated with the Communist Party. From its legislative study of the Communist Party, Congress concluded that that kind of activity was potentially dangerous to the national interest and that it must be subjected to control. But whatever the source from which the legislative experience and instruction derived, the Act applies to a class of activity only, not to the Communist Party as such. Nothing in this offends the constitutional prohibition of attainder.

B. *The Freedoms of Expression and Association Protected by the First Amendment.* The Communist Party would have us hold that the First Amendment prohibits Congress from requiring the registration and filing of information, including membership lists, by organizations substantially dominated or controlled by the foreign powers controlling the world Communist movement and which operate primarily to advance the objectives of that movement: the overthrow of existing government by any means necessary and the establishment in its place of a Communist totalitarian dictatorship. . . . We cannot find such a prohibition in the First Amendment. So to find would make a travesty of that Amendment and the great ends for the well-being of our democracy that it serves.

No doubt, a governmental regulation which requires registration as a condition upon the exercise of speech may in some circumstances affront the constitutional guarantee of free expression. . . . The present statute does not, of course, attach the registration requirement to the incident of speech, but to the incidents of foreign domination and of operation to advance the objectives of the world Communist movement—operation which, the Board has found here, includes extensive, long-continuing organizational, as well as "speech" activity. . . .

Similarly, we agree that compulsory disclosure of the names of an organization's members may in certain instances infringe constitutionally protected rights of association. . . . But to say this much is only to recognize one of the points of reference from which analysis must begin. To state that individual liberties may be affected is to establish the condition for, not to arrive at the conclusion of, constitutional decision. Against the impediments which particular governmental regulation causes to entire freedom of individual action, there must be weighed the value to the public of the ends which the regulation may achieve. . . .

Of course congressional power in this sphere, as in all spheres, is limited by the First Amendment. Individual liberties fundamental to American institutions are not to be destroyed under pretext of preserving those institutions, even from the gravest external dangers. But where the problems of accommodating the exigencies of self-preservation and the values of liberty are as complex and intricate as they are in the situation described in the findings of sec. 2 of the Subversive Activities Control Act—when existing government is menaced by a world-wide integrated movement which employs every combination of possible means, peaceful and violent, domestic and foreign, overt and clandestine, to destroy the government itself—the legislative judgment as to how that threat may best be met consistently with the safeguarding of personal freedom is not to be set aside merely because the judgment of judges would, in the first instance, have chosen other methods. Especially where Congress, in seeking to reconcile competing and urgently demanding values within our social institutions, legislates not to prohibit individuals from organizing for the effectuation of ends found to be menacing to the very existence of those institutions, but only to prescribe the conditions under which such organization is permitted, the legislative determination must be respected. . . .

. . . In light of [the legislature's] findings, based on voluminous evidence collected during years of investigation, we cannot say that that danger is chimerical, or that the registration requirement of sec. 7 is an ill-adjusted means of dealing with it. In saying this, we are not insensitive to the fact that . . . public opprobrium and obloquy . . . may attach to an individual listed with the Attorney General as a member of a Communist-action organization. But while an angry public opinion, and the evils which it may spawn, are relevant considerations in adjudging, in light of the totality of relevant considerations, the validity of legislation that, in effecting disclosure, may thereby entail some restraints on speech and association, the existence of an ugly public temper does not, as such and without more, incapacitate government to require publicity demanded by rational interests high in the scale of national concern. Where the mask of anonymity which an organization's members wear serves the double purpose of protecting them from popular prejudice and of enabling them to cover over a foreign-directed conspiracy, infiltrate into other groups and enlist the support of persons who would not, if the truth were revealed, lend their support . . . it would be a distortion of the First Amendment to hold that it prohibits Congress from removing the mask.

These considerations lead us to sustain the registration provisions of sec. 7, as not repugnant to the First Amendment, insofar as they require Communist-action organizations to file a registration statement containing the names and addresses of its present officers and members. . . .

It is argued that if Congress may constitutionally enact legislation requiring the Communist Party to register, to list its members, to file financial statements, and to identify its printing presses, Congress may impose similar requirements upon any group which pursues unpopular political objectives or which expresses an unpopular political ideology. Nothing which we decide here remotely carries such an implication. The Subversive Activities Control Act applies only to *foreign-dominated* organizations which work primarily to advance the objectives of a world movement controlled by the government of a *foreign* country. . . . It applies only to organizations directed, dominated, or controlled by a *particular* foreign country, the leader of a movement which, Congress has found, is "in its origins, its development, and its present practice, . . . a world-wide revolutionary movement whose purpose it is, by treachery, deceit, infiltration into other groups . . ., espionage, sabotage, terrorism, and any other means deemed necessary, to establish a Communist totalitarian dictatorship in the countries throughout the world through the medium of a world-wide Communist organization." . . . This is the full purported reach of the statute, and its fullest effect. There is no attempt here to impose stifling obligations upon the proponents of a particular political creed as such, or even to check the importation of particular political ideas from abroad for propagation here. The Act compels the registration of organized groups which have been made the instruments of a long-continued, systematic, disciplined activity directed by a foreign power and purposing to overthrow existing government in this country. Organizations are subject to it only when shown, after administrative hearing subject to judicial review, to be dominated by the foreign power or its organs and to operate primarily to advance its purposes. That a portion of the evidence upon which such a showing is made may consist in the expression of political views by the organization does not alter the character of the Act or of the incidents to which it attaches. Such expressions are relevant only as probative of foreign control and of the purposes to which the organization's actions are directed. The Board, in the present proceeding, so understood the Act. The registration requirement of sec. 7, on its face and as here applied, doe not violate the First Amendment.

C. *Self-Incrimination of the Party's Officers.*

. . . There is nothing in the case which justifies advisory adjudication of self-incrimination questions prior to the time when a demand for information has been, at the least, made and resisted.

D. *Legislative Predetermination of Adjudicative Fact.* It is next asserted that the Act offends the Due Process Clause of the Fifth Amendment. . . .

We find that nothing in this violates due process. . . .

Whether the particular organization against whom the Attorney General files a petition for a registration order operates primarily to advance those objectives [of Sec. 3] is the pertinent issue under the statute, and this issue may be litigated. That is all that due process requires. . . .

The other constitutional questions raised by the Party have been carefully considered, but do not call for detailed discussion. And we must decline, of course, to enter into discussion of the wisdom of this legislation. The Constitution does not prohibit the requirement that the Communist Party register with the Attorney General as a Communist-action organization pursuant to Section 7.

The judgment of the Court of Appeals is

Affirmed.

MR. CHIEF JUSTICE WARREN, *dissenting.*

I agree . . . that, once having entered the area of constitutional adjudication, the Court must decide now whether the Act violates the Fifth Amendment privilege against self-incrimination by requiring the petitioner's officers to submit a registration statement on behalf of the petitioner. . . . I believe that the Act does constitute a violation of the Fifth Amendment.

MR. JUSTICE BLACK, *dissenting.*

The Court's opinion is devoted chiefly to the task of explaining why it will not decide any of the substantial issues raised by this attack upon the constitutionality of the Act as it is actually written and will actually operate and why it must decide the case just as though none of these other burdens existed and we were dealing with an Act that required nothing more than the registration of an organization. I cannot agree to decide the case on any such hypothetical basis. If registration were the only issue in the case, I would agree at once that

Congress has power to require every "person" acting as an agent of a foreign principal to file registration statements comprehensively showing his agency activities as is required, for example, by the Foreign Agents Registration Act. . . .

The Act before us now, however, . . . is not based on the principle that "our people, adequately informed, may be trusted to distinguish between the true and the false." Instead, the present Act, like many other pieces of current legislation, is based on the precisely contrary principle that "our people (even when) adequately informed, may (not) be trusted to distinguish between the true and the false." In this regard, the principle upon which Congress acted in passing the Subversive Activities Control Act is identical to that upon which it acted in making membership in the Communist Party a crime in the Smith Act, a provision under which the Court has today sustained the conviction and imprisonment for six years of a person for being a mere member of the Communist Party with knowledge of its purposes. [See Scales case.] Statutes based upon such a principle, which really amounts to nothing more than the idea that the Government must act as a paternal guardian to protect American voters from hearing public policies discussed, do not implement "the prized freedoms guaranteed by the First Amendment"—they are designed to and do directly detract from those freedoms. . . .

The plan of the Act is to make it impossible for an organization to continue to function once a registration order is issued against it. To this end, the Act first provides crushing penalties to insure complete compliance with the disclosure requirements of registration. Thus, if the Party or its members fail to register within the time required by the Act, or if they fail to make annual reports as required, or to keep records as required, each individual guilty of such failure can be punished by a fine of $10,000, by imprisonment for five years, or both, for each offense—and each offense means "each day of failure to register" or "each listing of the name or address of any one individual" either by the organization or by an individual. Thus, for a delay of thirty days in filing required reports, a fine of $300,000 and imprisonment for 150 years could be imposed by a trial judge.

Having thus made it mandatory that Communist organizations and individual Communists make a full disclosure of their identities and activities, the Act then proceeds to heap burden after burden upon those so exposed. Certain tax deductions allowed to others are denied to a registered organization. Mail matter must be stamped before the organization sends it out to show that it was disseminated by a "Communist action" organization, with all the treasonable connotations given that term by the recitals of "fact" in the Act. Members of a registered organization cannot hold certain jobs with the Government, or any jobs with private businesses engaged in doing certain work for the Government. Members cannot use or attempt to use a passport and cannot even make application for a passport without being subject to a penalty of five years in the penitentiary. The Act thus makes it extremely difficult for a member of the Communist Party to live in this country and, at the same time, makes it a crime for him to try to get a passport to get out.

In addition to these burdens imposed directly by the Act itself, the registration requirement must also be considered in the context of the other laws not existing which affect the Communist Party. The

Act requires that the information obtained upon registration be given wide publicity thus insuring that those identified as members of the Party will be subjected to all the civil disabilities, criminal prosecutions and public harassments that have become common in recent years. I agree with Mr. Justice Douglas that this aspect of the Act is alone sufficient to establish its invalidity under the self-incrimination provision of the Fifth Amendment. But I think the interrelationship between the present Act and these other laws goes deeper than that, for I think that interrelationship establishes all but conclusively that the present Act cannot be upheld as a mere registration statute. The information elicited by the Act must be considered, not, as in the Viereck case, an aid to the exercise of individual judgment by the people, but rather a part of a pattern of suppression by the Government, for that is certainly the inevitable effect of any system that requires registration on the one hand and imposes pains and penalties upon those registering on the other.

All of these enormous burdens, which are necessarily imposed upon the Party and its members by the act of registration, are dismissed by the Court on the basis of an alleged conflict with the Court-created rule that constitutional questions should be avoided whenever possible. Thus, the Court engages in extended discussions as to whether the people involved will ever want to do the things the Act says they cannot do and whether they will ever object to doing the things the Act says they must do, suggesting, among other things, that the members of the Communist Party may never object to providing the evidence needed to send them to prison for violating the Smith Act; that they may never protest because they are forced to give up the tax deduc-

tions that other people receive; that they may be willing to stamp all the Party's mail as coming from an evil organization; that they may never want to hold the jobs from which the Act disqualifies them; and that they may never want to get a passport to get out of the country. On the basis of all these "uncertainties" the Court seems to consider its hands tied because, it says, these are as yet only potential impairments of constitutional rights. In its view, there is no "justiciable" issue at all between the United States and the Communist Party except the bare requirement of registration.

In the context of this case, I can find no justification for the Court's refusal to pass upon the serious constitutional questions raised. . . . The only sense in which the Court has avoided a constitutional issue is by permitting the destruction of a group seeking to raise the issue of the constitutionality of its destruction.

This whole Act, with its pains and penalties, embarks this country, for the first time, on the dangerous adventure of outlawing groups that preach doctrines nearly all Americans detest. When the practice of outlawing parties and various public groups begins, no one can say where it will end. In most countries such a practice once begun ends with a one-party government. There is something of tragic irony in the fact that this Act, expressly designed to protect this Nation from becoming a "totalitarian dictatorship" with "a single political party" has adopted to achieve its laudable purpose the policy of outlawing a party—a policy indispensable to totalitarian dictatorships. I think we should meet and decide this whole question now in the administration of a sound judicial policy that carries out our responsibilities both to Congress and to the American people.

In my judgment, the Act here under

consideration is unconstitutional on at least three grounds in addition to its direct conflict with the self-incrimination provisions of the Fifth Amendment. It is, in the first instance, a classical bill of attainder which our Constitution in two places prohibits, for it is a legislative act that inflicts pains, penalties and punishments in a number of ways without a judicial trial. The legislative fact-findings as to Communist activities, which the Court—despite the constitutional command for trial of such facts by a court and jury—accepts as facts, supply practically all of the proof needed to bring the Communist Party within the proscriptions of the Act. The Act points unerringly to the members of that Party as guilty people who must be penalized as the Act provides. At the same time, these legislative fact-findings fall little short of being adequate in themselves to justify a finding of guilt against any person who can be identified, however faintly, by any informer, as ever having been a member of the Communist Party. Most of whatever is lacking in the legislative fact-findings is later supplied by administrative fact-findings of an agency which is not a court, which is not manned by independent judges, and which does not have to observe the constitutional right to trial by jury and other trial safeguards unequivocally commanded by the Bill of Rights. Yet, after this agency has made its findings and its conclusions, neither its findings of fact nor the findings of fact of the legislative body can subsequently be challenged in court by any individual who may later be brought up on a charge that he failed to register as required by the Act and the Board. The Act thus not only is a legislative bill of attainder but also violates due process by short-cutting practically all of the Bill of Rights, leaving no hope for anyone entangled in this legislative-administrative web except what has proved in this case to be one of the most truncated judicial reviews that the history of this Court can afford.

I think also that this outlawry of the Communist Party and imprisonment of its members violates the First Amendment. The question under that Amendment is whether Congress has power to outlaw an association, group or party either on the ground that it advocates a policy of violent overthrow of the existing government at some time in the distant future or on the ground that it is ideologically subservient to some foreign country. In my judgment, neither of these factors justifies an invasion of rights protected by the First Amendment. Talk about the desirability of revolution has a long and honorable history, not only in other parts of the world, but in our own country. This kind of talk, like any other, can be used at the wrong time and for the wrong purpose. But, under our system of Government, the remedy for this danger must be the same remedy that is applied to the danger that comes from any other erroneous talk—education and contrary argument. If that remedy is not sufficient, the only meaning of free speech must be that the revolutionary ideas will be allowed to prevail.

This conclusion is not affected by the fact that those advocating a policy of revolution are in sympathy with a foreign government. If there is one thing certain about the First Amendment it is that this Amendment was designed to guarantee the freest interchange of ideas about all public matters and that, of course, means the interchange of *all* ideas, however such ideas may be viewed in other countries and whatever change in the existing structure of government it may be hoped that these ideas will bring about. Now, when this country is trying to spread the high ideals of democracy all over the world—ideals that are revolutionary in many countries—seems to be a particularly inappropriate time to stifle First Amendment freedoms in this country. The same arguments that are used to justify the outlawry of Communist ideas here could be used to justify an outlawry of the ideas of democracy in other countries. . . .

I would reverse this case and leave the Communists free to advocate their beliefs in proletarian dictatorship publicly and openly among the people of this country with full confidence that the people will remain loyal to any democratic Government truly dedicated to freedom and justice—the kind of Government which some of us still think of as being "the last best hope of earth."

MR. JUSTICE DOUGLAS *also dissented.* MR. JUSTICE BRENNAN *dissented in part.*

[NOTE: On the basis of this ruling, the Department of Justice brought a suit in the District Court in December, 1962 against the Communist Party for failure to register. The Party was found guilty and fined $120,000.00. This verdict was then appealed. On December 17, 1963, the United States Court of Appeals in a unanimous decision reversed the finding of the District Court on the grounds that there was no person available who would run the risk of incriminating himself to register in behalf of the Party. It is now up to the Department of Justice to take further action.]

III. THE COMMUNIST PARTY AND THE CONSTITUTION: A CONTROVERSY

At the close of World War II, most Americans hoped that the United States and the Soviet Union would continue the cooperation that had made possible the establishment of the United Nations and the victory over Germany and Japan. The period of cooperation was brief. By the middle of 1950, the Soviet Union was in control of all Eastern Europe with the exception of West Berlin, which had survived, in 1948, the first of many blockades. The Chinese mainland was ruled by Mao Tse-tung, and the North Koreans had begun an invasion of South Korea. And, by the middle of 1950, the apparent polarization of power in the world was reflected domestically in the United States by a tendency to discuss all political issues in terms of Communism or anti-Communism. In March of 1947, President Truman ordered an investigation of the loyalty of employees of the Executive Branch. In August of 1948, Whittaker Chambers accused Alger Hiss, an official of the Department of State, of secret membership in the Communist Party. The next few years saw the conviction of eleven Communist leaders under the Smith Act (14 October 1949), the conviction of Hiss on charges of perjury (21 January 1950), the conviction of Judith Coplon of espionage (7 March 1950), the rise to national notoriety of Senator Joseph McCarthy, the indictment of Julius and Ethel Rosenberg on charges of espionage (August 1950),[1] and the passage, over President Truman's veto, of the McCarran Act (23 September 1950). By the end of 1950, the constitutional status of the Communist Party had become one of the major issues of American politics.

In response to what seemed at times a combination of fear and fanaticism, Alan Barth and a number of others spoke out on behalf of civil liberties. Barth's book, The Loyalty of Free Men *(1950), was a defense of freedom of thought and action, and a warning of the dangers attached to the Government's loyalty and security programs. Irving Kristol, editor of* Commentary, *was among the many liberals and socialists who felt that Barth and others had understated the dangers of subversion. Kristol's arguments were answered in a lengthy rejoinder from Alan F. Westin, a Columbia professor who was then a teaching fellow at Harvard. Taken together, these two articles are an excellent introduction to the general problem within which the specific problems posed by the Smith and McCarran Acts are central.*

---

[1] The Rosenbergs were subsequently, after much controversy and agitation, put to death. [Editor's note.]

Irving Kristol: "CIVIL LIBERTIES," 1952—A STUDY IN CONFUSION

Heard ye not lately of a man
That went beside his witt,
And naked through the citty rann
Wrapt in a frantique fitt?

THE above tantalizing bit of 17th-century verse was quoted recently in the London *Times Literary Supplement*, in the same issue in which there appeared, elsewhere in its pages, a review of the English edition of Alan Barth's *The Loyalty of Free Men*. This fortuitous juxtaposition was not without its ironic relevance, Mr. Barth's book having been provoked by the "frantique fitt" of McCarthyism, beneath which he saw a cool and calculating assault on the American democracy, and his defense being couched in a cool and calculating eloquence that turns out, upon close examination, to be not nearly the exercise in pure reason it seems.

A close examination, however, Mr. Barth's book and others of its kind have not received. It was hardly to be expected from Senator McCarthy and his friends, who are less famous for their habits of meticulous reading than for their preference for arguing in the large, while the more scholarly sections of American opinion have been so delighted to see the Senator get his, and so soothed by the cadences of a familiar tone, that they have not so much read these books as permitted themselves to be enchanted by them. This enchantment has had its political sequel, for as a result of it there has been drawn a line of battle. On the one side are the men of intellect and sensibility, fair-minded and generous-hearted and confessedly not infallible: the Alan Barths, the Henry Steele Com-

magers, the Zechariah Chafees, the Howard Mumford Joneses, the Ralph Barton Perrys, the William O. Douglases, and, rather more tentatively committed, the Francis Biddles. On the other side are the mindless men, the kind who get elected to office when the spirit of the age reverts to primitivism, and who wish, under cover of fighting Communism, to squeeze the nation into a Know-Nothing straitjacket.

The line is drawn—and those liberals who have rallied to their positions on the left of it find themselves ever more pressed against the outer walls of the city. The ready quotations from Jefferson about the trees of liberty and the blood of tryants, the sonorous repetition of Justice Holmes' dissenting opinions, the schoolmaster's measured accents alternating with prophetic indignation—the whole battery has failed significantly to make an impression on the dominant American mood. Senator McCarthy remains blithely on the offensive and his critics give ground before him. It is a most exasperating and melancholy situation for liberals to be in; yet in proportion as they fail in strength, they gain in their sense of petulant righteousness.

Is it conceivable that the line was incorrectly drawn in the first place? The liberals are loath to weigh the possibility lest it give comfort to the enemy; Senator McCarthy for his part has no cause for dissatisfaction with things as they are; but those of us who are the displaced persons of this war might reflect on this question to our advantage. Perhaps it is a calamitous error to believe that because a vulgar demagogue lashes out at both Communism and liberalism as identical,

Reprinted with permission from *Commentary*, XXX (March 1952), pp. 228-36. Copyright 1952, American Jewish Committee.

it is necessary to protect Communism in order to defend liberalism. This way of putting the matter will surely shock liberals, who are convinced that it is only they who truly understand Communism and who thoughtfully oppose it. They are nonetheless mistaken, and it is a mistake on which McCarthyism waxes fat. For there is one thing that the American people know about Senator McCarthy: he, like them, is unequivocally anti-Communist. About the spokesmen for American liberalism, they feel they know no such thing. And with some justification.

With what justification, can be seen from an illustrative incident involving Professor Henry Steele Commager, a distinguished historian who never was a Communist and never will be. In the May 1947 issue of *Harper's*, Professor Commager wrote a spirited article that began as follows:

"On May 6 a Russian-born girl, Mrs. Shura Lewis, gave a talk to the students of the Western High School of Washington, D.C. She talked about Russia—its school system, its public health program, the position of women, of the aged, of the workers, the farmers, and the professional classes—and compared, superficially and uncritically, some American and Russian institutions. . . . Mrs. Lewis said nothing that had not been said a thousand times, in speeches, in newspapers, magazines and books. She said nothing that any normal person could find objectionable."

What greatly disturbed Professor Commager was that this inoffensive speech did give rise to a furor in Washington. Congressmen bellowed that our schools were being subverted, the principal of the school came forward with a humble apology, the superintendent of schools for the nation's capital swore it would never happen again, and the speech itself was reprinted (after some discussion of the wisdom of exposing the public to inflammation) in the Congressional Record as a horrible example. Professor Commager saw in this a reflection of an anti-Communist hysteria that threatened to engulf all civil liberties, and he pleaded earnestly that reason control the anti-Communist passion, lest we find ourselves saddled with an anti-Communist orthodoxy no less reprehensible than the Communist one. His article was hailed as a kind of liberal manifesto, and was reprinted—alongside John Stuart Mill and John Milton—in Howard Mumford Jones' *Primer of Intellectual Freedom* (1949). Evil won a transient victory in the seats of power and Good won a permanent niche in the anthologies—a familiar tale.

Familiar, that is, until one goes to the Congressional Record and reads through this speech that no "normal person could find objectionable." Mrs. Lewis' English was broken, but her sentiments were whole:

"They call it collective farm—the peasants farm and divide up products according to work put in by each individual during the year. As a result of planning, unemployment is completely wiped out. . . .

"In Russia right now people absolutely do not worry about today or tomorrow. They never think 'All of a sudden I lose a job.' That fear doesn't exist among Russian people. . . .

"No matter where you live you have to work. What the Russian people have, they are more secure about this. They work. They need not worry much about losing the job. They are free to travel from one place to another, and each person must work 25 years for after that he is able to get a pension. No matter where you work—in this plant or another,

25 years and then you get 50% of your salary and live the rest of your life. . . .

"I never appreciated the life in Russia until I live here. Here you have to work hard in order to live, use all your courage not to die. . . .

"I read all the papers here and occasionally I go to the Library of Congress and read all papers printed in Moscow. It is very interesting, and when I read these papers always you can see here evidence of press where people talk all the time about having a war, to throw the atomic bomb on Russia, to destroy because they have a system which is very prideful. At the present time Russians are busy to restore all those houses, ,all those cities, all those towns. Russian people make streets, plants, produce new style of shoes, new fashion of dress, new production, and never they talk about having a war."

The echoes this awakened in Congress may have been exaggerated, but they were not factitious or beside the point. Obviously, Professor Commager can argue that it will not harm American school children to encounter an occasional Communist apologist in the flesh; one may even go further and say it would do them good. However, in the first place, Mrs. Lewis was not introduced as a Communist apologist but as an informed reporter, and, in the second place, everything she said should have been objectionable to every normal person, and especially to a historian like Professor Commager—for the good and sufficient reason that it was a tissue of lies. For Professor Commager to defend the rights of Communists to free speech is one thing, for him to assert that there is nothing objectionable in mendacious pleading in support of Communism is quite another. The conclusion "any normal person" will draw from such behav-

ior is that, for whatever reason, his critical faculties are less alert when he looks out of the left corner of his eye.

Indeed, the heart of the matter is exactly that he looks at Communism out of the *left* corner of his eye. Professor Commager seems to be seduced by the insidious myth according to which Communism is a political trend continuous with liberalism and democratic socialism, only more impatient and inclined to the fanatical, only more "radical" than its companions who are not quite so "left." It is a myth that Senator McCarthy, for his own ends, is happy to accept, since it allows him to tag a New Dealer as being by nature an embryonic Communist. Neither the Professor nor the Senator is concerned to see that the antithesis of "left" and "right" no longer suits the political realities; that measured by the ideals of the French or even Russian Revolution, Communism today is as counter-revolutionary as Louis XVI or Kolchak ever was; that if one wishes to defend the civil liberties of Communists (as the Senator does not), one must do so on the same grounds that one defends the civil liberties of Nazis and fascists—no more, no less.

Professor Commager might retort that he knows all this full well, and that he is for civil liberties for everyone, fascist, Communist, or what-have-you. But if a Nazi had, in 1938, addressed a high-school audience in this country, extolling the accomplishments of Hitler's regime, presenting a thoroughly fictitious account of life in Nazi Germany, never once mentioning the existence of concentration camps—would Professor Commager find in such a speech "nothing that any normal person could find objectionable"? It is doubtless an injustice to him even to conceive of the possibility.

This notion of Communism as "left"

and therefore at an opposite pole from fascism, which is "right," appears to have become intrinsic to the liberal outlook. It is imbedded in the meretricious historical analogies, in the rolling phrases about "the forces of freedom and those of fear," beneath which there lies the gross metaphysic of the liberal Manichee, apportioning the universe to "forward-looking" and "backward-looking" demi-urges. It helps explain how Professor Commager can permit himself to write: "After all, it is no accident that the nations dedicated to freedom won the two great wars of the 20th century and those committed to totalitarianism went under"—when it is not only no accident, it is not even a fact. The same notion is evidenced in Zechariah Chafee's explanation (in his essay in the recent symposium *Civil Liberties Under Attack*) of the origin of Communist fronts: "It is inevitable that the membership of organizations formed to bring about change should include some persons who want a great deal of change"—as if Professor Chafee and the Communists were agreed on the direction of the change, quarreling only over the measure. It is the presupposition from which Ralph Barton Perry (in his new book *The Citizen Decides*) can deduce that Communism is "democratic" by virtue of being a revolt of the "masses" against the "classes," that the Soviet regime is a government "for the people with the consent of the people" though not by the people, and that the Chinese Communist leaders are "hostages" of a popular revolution.

Moreover, after staring out of the left corner of the eye for any length of time, there comes an irrepressible inclination to wink. How else explain, for instance, the attitude Alan Barth takes toward the Hiss-Chambers affair? He can begin a sentence: "Insofar as Chambers may be credited with having told the truth. . . .";

or: "whatever the guilt of Alger Hiss and whatever the utility of exposing it and punishing it a decade later. . . ." About Whittaker Chambers and the Communist "informer" in general, he is no longer judiciously bland but is knowingly tart: "The ex-Communists, conscious of their betrayal of American values, wanted the comfort of company; they had to show that many others, even many who were highly respected, had been as recreant as they." In other words, Chambers in telling the truth is a man of malice, Hiss in denying it is his defenseless victim. Hiss's guilt is problematic and, in any case, not important; Chambers' wickedness is certain.

On Owen Lattimore, there is liberal unanimity: he got a raw deal. Professor Commager believes (in his contribution to *Civil Liberties Under Attack*) that the attack on Lattimore was an attack on "independence and non-conformity." Professor Chafee laments: "Owen Lattimore did his own thinking and look how his services were appreciated." Alan Barth is casually positive: "Dr. Lattimore's ordeal was, of course, only the most spectacular instance of legislative punishment of teachers for expressing their opinions." About the worst that can be said for such arrant nonsense is that it is uttered in all sincerity. For the incontrovertible facts of the case are, "of course," that Owen Lattimore did *not* do his own thinking; that his "ordeal" was the public demonstration of this fact; that he was a faithful and enormously influential fellow-traveler who for more than a decade followed the Communist line as if magnetized by it, including a docile zig-zag during the Stalin-Hitler pact. Is it really no legitimate concern of Congress that such a man was appointed advisor to Chiang Kai-shek, that he accompanied Vice-President Wallace during his tour of Asia, that he was admired and listened to by important people in the State Department?

In his denunciation of Lattimore's pro-Communist record and in hurling unsubstantiated charges against him (chief of Soviet espionage, etc.), Senator McCarthy may well have been aiming a blow against independence of mind and nonconformity of spirit. For Messrs. Commager, Barth, and Chafee to defend Lattimore's pro-Communist record in order to defend such independence and nonconformity, is for them to play the Senator's game, on the losing side.

It is equally futile for liberals to try to match Senator McCarthy's irresponsible declamations with a crafty rhetoric of their own, especially when this rhetoric, while not designedly pro-Communist, is compelled by the logic of disingenuousness and special pleading to become so in effect. The need for disingenuousness arises out of a refusal to see Communism for what it is: a movement guided by conspiracy and aiming at totalitarianism, rather than merely another form of "dissent" or "nonconformity." Hence the liberal argument runs askew of reality and must clothe itself with neat obfuscation.

Once again, Professor Commager obliges with a superior specimen:

"The House Un-American Activities Committee has launched an attack on the Lawyers' Guild as a pro-Communist or 'subversive' organization. The chief basis for this attack is, as far as we know, that the Guild has proffered its services to the defense of Communists under indictment for violation of the Smith Act. We need not inquire into the accuracy of this charge or into the degree of zeal displayed by the Lawyers' Guild. Let us ask rather what are the logical conclusions to be drawn by the position which the

House Committee has adopted? They are two: that certain criminals are so despicable that they are not entitled to counsel, and that a lawyer who defends a criminal is himself sympathetic to crime."

That phrase in the second sentence, "as far as we know," is curious. It implies strongly that the only conceivable explanation of the Committee's attitude is the action of the Guild in providing lawyers to defend indicted Communists, and that there is no public information which gives plausibility to the Committee's belief that the Guild is a "front" organization, controlled and run by Communists. On the contrary, however, "as far as we know," and we know much further than Professor Commager suggests, the Lawyers' Guild is a Communist creation that, as A. A. Berle stated when he resigned from it in 1940, "is not prepared to take any stand which conflicts with the Communist party line." Moreover, the House Committee on Un-American Activities has collected and published sufficient evidence to demonstrate this beyond cavil—which leads one to think that if Professor Commager spent nearly as much time reading the records of Congressional hearings as he does denouncing them, we should all be better off.

The entire third sentence is even more curious: "We need not inquire into the accuracy of this charge or into the degree of zeal displayed by the Lawyers' Guild." If we take "zeal" to mean pro-Communism (in the context, that is all it can mean), then the degree of this zeal and the accuracy of the charge of pro-Communism are precisely what we *do* need to inquire into. How can we know whether to sanction or condemn the Committee's investigation of the Guild as a pro-Communist organization unless we make an effort to find out if the Guild is or is not, in fact, a pro-Communist organization? Even Professor Commager surreptitiously ignores his own disclaimer, as the last two sentences of his paragraph show. Obviously, the two "logical conclusions" flow, not from the Committee's premise, but his own: namely, that the Lawyers' Guild is neither pro-Communist nor subversive. From the Committee's own premise, other quite logical conclusions may be inferred—one of them being that the Committee is engaged in showing up Communist fronts for what they are. Professor Commager's "logic" is a slight-of-hand whereby premises that are prejudiced in favor of the Communist interpretation of affairs are made to pass for natural conclusions.

In the same vein, there is a liberal rhetoric of insinuation that works under cover of a high moral posture. Its net effect is to give a backhanded credence to the Communist assertion that it is impossible to oppose Communism vigorously without walking into the arms of Black Reaction. It is the kind of thing represented in the following observation of Alan Barth's:

"In the New York trial of eleven Communist Party leaders in 1949, a number of FBI undercover operatives who had joined the party appeared as prosecution witnesses. How widely such agents have been dispersed in labor unions, in lawful voluntary associations, and in political groups is a matter of mere conjecture. But it is certainly a matter of legitimate concern to Americans who care about preservation of the traditional rights of privacy."

A noble sentiment, and the unwary reader assents—who is against the right to privacy, and who is not prepared to be concerned with its violation? Only the exceptionally attentive will note that the supposed threat to "the traditional

rights of privacy" is "a matter of mere conjecture." Whose conjecture? We are not told. Is there any ground for such a conjecture? We are not told that either. Is Mr. Barth against the use of undercover agents in principle? He does not say so. Is he against the use of undercover agents in Communist organizations? He does not say this, either. He would seem to be against dispersing FBI agents in bona fide labor unions, lawful voluntary associations, and political groups, and reminds us of the consequences. But who is for it? The answer, which he does not bother to give, is: nobody—and that is why the FBI is doing no such thing and why the whole business is a "matter of mere conjecture." In the course of Mr. Barth's innuendoes, however, the onus has been neatly shifted from the Communist conspirators to the FBI agents who identified them.

The same technique of persuasion is at work in such a statement as this one by Professor Commager: "It will be useful to determine, a generation from now, whether those universities that have purged their faculties are actually stronger than they were before the purges occurred—stronger in those essentials that go to make a university." This has about it so trembling an air of bittersweet wisdom that it seems positively boorish to ask: just which universities would Professor Commager describe as "purged"? Surely Columbia is not one of them, for Professor Commager is not the kind of man who would retain his post on a "purged" faculty. Is it Yale? Princeton? Harvard? University of Chicago? The list could be extended indefinitely, and never provoke an affirmative response, for there is not a single university in the United States that can be said to have been, in any meaningful sense of the word, "purged." There has been no more than a handful of cases where Communist college teachers have been dismissed, and less than a handful of cases where non-Communists have been unjustly fired as "Reds." To call this a "purge"—even regardless of whether or not one thinks Communists have a right to teach in colleges—is to echo Communist propaganda.

Perhaps Professor Commager had in mind the University of California, where several dozen (out of a total of more than a thousand) teachers found the idea of a special loyalty oath—the content of which was irrelevant to their action—so offensive and intolerable that they exercised their constitutional right to refuse to swear it, and consequently had to seek other employment. Granting that the notion of a special oath for teachers is obnoxious, and even conceding that this minority was correct and courageous in its particular reaction to it—is it the part of sobriety to insist, as Professor Commager goes on to do, that the philosophy behind the actions of California's Board of Trustees does not differ "in any essentials" from the philosophy behind the totalitarian control of university teaching? One swallow does not make a spring, or one injustice an apocalypse.

Despite their fondness for clichés of Communist manufacture, all these liberal spokesmen are sincerely anti-Communist—otherwise, what they have to say would be of little interest to anyone. But their rejection of Communism has all the semblance of a preliminary gesture, a repudiation aiming to linger in the memory as a floating credential. It has little relation to all the ensuing scenes of the political drama, where bad conscience and stubborn pride join to guide the liberal through his role.

Did not the major segment of American liberalism, as a result of joining hands with the Communists in a Popular Front, go on record as denying the existence of Soviet concentration camps? Did it not give its blessing to the "liquidation" of millions of Soviet "kulaks"? Did it not apologize for the mass purges of 1936-38, and did it not solemnly approve the grotesque trials of the Old Bolsheviks? Did it not applaud the massacre of the non-Communist left by the GPU during the Spanish Civil War? All this carries no weight with Alan Barth who knows that, though a man repeat the Big Lie, so long as he is of a liberal intention he is saved. On the participation of non-Communists in Communist fronts during the 30's, he writes: "In the main, their participation, while it lasted, was not only innocent but *altogether* praiseworthy." (My italics.)

Even Francis Biddle, who is generally cautious, remarks in his book *The Fear of Freedom:* "What makes an organization subversive? If a vast majority of its members are Communists but its conduct has always been exemplary, advocating desirable social reforms which Communists usually back, it can hardly fit the description."

One surmises that Mr. Biddle is not really so politically naive as this statement, on the face of it, would lead one to believe. He must know what it means to be "subversive," since it was he who, as Attorney General, sent eighteen members of a minuscule Trotskyist sect to jail in 1942 for being just that; he must know how Communists work, how front organizations act as an ancillary to the Communist party apparatus, since this is a matter of common knowledge and Mr. Biddle is uncommonly literate and intelligent. No, it was no elevated unsophistication that urged him on, but rather a sense of shame and a cowardliness to confess that shame. Mr. Biddle, like Mr. Barth, refuses to admit what is now apparent: that a generation of earnest reformers who helped give this country a New Deal should find themselves in retrospect stained with the guilt of having lent aid and comfort to Stalinist tyranny. This is, to be sure, a truth of hindsight, an easy truth. But it is the truth nonetheless, and might as well be owned up to. If American liberalism is not willing to discriminate between its achievements and its sins, it only disarms itself before Senator McCarthy, who is eager to have it appear that its achievements *are* its sins.

There is a false pride, by which liberals persuade themselves that no matter what association a man has had with a Communist enterprise, he is absolutely guiltless of the crimes that Communism has committed so long as he was moved to this association by a generous idealism. There is a political mythology, by which liberals locate Communism over on the "left," in a zone exempt from the unsparing verdict directed against the totalitarian "right." There is also a fear, a fear that the American democracy in an excess of anti-Communism will gather its abundant energy into a wave of "conformism" that will drown all free thought. This pride, this mythology, this fear all unite for a liberal prejudgment of issues (e.g., the cases of Alger Hiss, Owen Lattimore, William Remington, Harry Dexter White) which is not easy to explain on a purely rational view. It is what stimulates a flood of irrelevant and gaudy prose about loyalty in the abstract ("like love it must be given freely," etc.) while it shuns a careful discussion of Communist disloyalty in the concrete.

Of the three factors, the fear of "conformism" or "orthodoxy" is probably the most influential in its appeal, for it is founded in some degree on objective fact. Alexis de Tocqueville and John Stuart Mill, both friendly critics of the egalitarian trend, pointed out long ago that in every democratic society there is an inherent tendency toward a "despotism of public opinion"; where the majority makes the laws, it may also wish—especially in feverish and unsettled times—to make opinion, lauding the popular and extirpating the unpopular. In America, where the people are more powerful than elsewhere, and where there is, too, a significant tradition of vigilante-ism, the danger of a despotism of public opinion is proportionately greater. When the State Department is forced to suspend an exhibition abroad of modern American art because some Congressmen denounce it as "Communistic," the danger of such a despotism seems more than academic, and many otherwise sensible people are led to reprehend any attempt to unveil Communist activities or Communist beliefs as a malignant form of "punishment by publicity," which will soon be extended to all opinions that illiterate and narrow-minded Congressmen detest.

What these people do not see is that Communism, because it is a conspiratorial movement, has not the faintest interest in any genuine resistance to the despotism of public opinion. These martyrs whose testament is—"I refuse to answer on the grounds that it might incriminate me"! These "intellectuals" of Hollywood and radio who are outraged at a Congressman's insistence that they say what they actually believe, and who wail that they are in danger of—being excluded from well-paying jobs! Is this the vibrant voice of "nonconformity" and "dissent"? Are these the American rebels of today? Oddly enough, the majority of American liberals seem to think so:

they have been moved to indignation by the questions, but never moved to disgust by the answers. Presumably, this is what they think a dissenter looks like, and no sadder commentary is possible on the corruption they have inflicted on themselves. And not only on themselves—for this image of a dissenter happens to coincide with the image held by Joseph McCarthy and Pat McCarran, for whom the dissenter is *per se* a scheming subversive. No greater spur to the despotism of public opinion can be imagined than this identification of free thought with underground conspiracy.

There is only one way the despotism of public opinion can be resisted. That is for a person with unpopular views to express himself, loudly, brazenly, stubbornly, in disregard of the consequences. Such a person may have to suffer for his convictions, as others have suffered before him, and as others will suffer after. But the responsibility for the mind's freedom in a democracy lies with the intransigent thinker, with his courage to shout the truth in the face of the mob, with his faith that truth will win out, and with his maddening commitment to the truth, win or lose. Yet, during all the occasions of the past several years, not a single liberal voice was to say to these strange "victims": "Speak up and damn the consequences! Let them take your job—as they certainly will anyway; tell the truth—you have nothing to lose and honor to gain!" Instead, there were erudite essays on the "right to a job" that would have corroborated William James in his mournful conviction that "the prevalent fear of poverty among our educated classes is the worst moral disease from which our civilization suffers."

Still, unworthy as these "victims" are, may they not, despite themselves, represent the right of the individual to hold whatever opinions he pleases without having to give a public accounting of them? Even if these Communists and Communist sympathizers are despicable, don't they have the right to believe privately anything they please? This is the way the question is frequently put, and it reveals a total misapprehension as to what Communism really is.

Communism is an Idea, beyond question. Indeed, it is an Idea, and it is of the essence of this Idea that it is also a conspiracy to subvert every social and political order it does not dominate. It is, furthermore, an Idea that has ceased to have any intellectual status but has become incarnate in the Soviet Union and the official Communist parties, to whose infallible directives unflinching devotion is owed. A person who is captive to this Idea can, at any time, in any place, be called upon to do whatever the Idea, i.e., the Party, thinks necessary. Since this is so, it is of considerably more than private interest if a person is held by the Idea—he is, all appearances to the contrary, a person with different loyalties, and with different canons of scrupulousness, from ours. To grant him an "immunity by silence" is to concede the right to conspiracy, a concession no government ever has made or ever will make.

This sounds exaggerated, as it must, being so foreign to the nature of American political experience. Many of us have known Communists, and most of them conveyed no impression of being conspirators. But then, some of us have known Nazis too, and they conveyed no immediate association with gas chambers. It is quite impossible to judge a political movement by the personality of an individual member. Roosevelt certainly didn't see in Stalin any symptoms of blood lust. Hermann Goering in jail struck one as a clever clown. And there are still plenty of people who can't believe that Alger Hiss ever did any such thing.

No doubt there are some present members of the Communist party who would, in a showdown, break free of the Idea and rally to the democratic cause. Unfortunately, we have no way of knowing who they are. No doubt there are some present members and fellow-travelers of the Communist party who would sooner or later get disillusioned with Communism if they were permitted to hold down their present jobs as teachers, civil service workers, etc., whereas they are likely to harden in the face of persecution. Unfortunately, it is quite as impossible to tell the citizens of Oshkosh, some of whom have suffered personal loss as a result of the war in Korea, that there is no harm in having their children taught the three R's by a Communist, as it would have been to persuade the citizens of Flatbush in 1939 that there was no cause for excitement in their children being taught by a Nazi, or to convince a businessman that it is a smart practice for him to pay a handsome salary to someone pledged to his "liquidation." No doubt some of these people became Communists after having suffered during the depression, or during a labor conflict, or, as a result of race prejudice, and society must bear its share of the blame. Unfortunately, as Fitzjames Stephens remarked many decades ago: "It does not follow that because society caused a fault it is not to punish it. A man who breaks his arm when he is drunk may have to cut it off when he is sober."

The problem of fighting Communism while preserving civil liberties is no simple one, and there is no simple solution. A prerequisite for any solution, however, is, firstly, a proper understanding of Communism for what it is, and

secondly, a sense of proportion. So long as liberals agree with Senator McCarthy that the fate of Communism involves the fate of liberalism, and that we must choose between complete civil liberties for everyone and a disregard for civil liberties entirely, we shall make no progress except to chaos. So long as one is either for or against "guilt by association," it is hopeless to try to distinguish between a sober and silly definition of that concept—sober when it is taken to mean, as for instance the Canwell Committee of the State of Washington took it to mean, that anyone who is a member of three or more organizations officially declared subversive is to be considered a Communist; silly when it is taken to mean, as many government loyalty boards take it to mean, that if you have a friend or a relation who is sympathetic to Communism, you are a "bad security risk." So long as Senator McCarthy and the liberals agree that the right of a Communist to teach or be a government employee is a matter of principle, we shall remain distant from that intelligent discrimination between one case and another, and one situation and another, which alone can give us our true bearings. And so long as Senator McCarthy and the liberals are enmeshed in this confusion, the Senator will grow the stronger, for such confusion is the sap of his political life.

Inevitably, liberals will disagree among themselves about the appropriateness of specific actions with regard to Communism and Communists. Inevitably, too, there will always be a basic division and antagonism between liberalism (which is solicitous of freedom) and McCarthyism (which is not). But if a liberal wishes to defend the civil liberties of Communists or of Communist fellow-travelers, he must enter the court of American opinion with clean hands and a clear mind. He must show that he knows the existence of an organized subversive movement such as Communism is a threat to the consensus on which civil society and its liberties are based. He must bluntly acknowledge Communists and fellow-travelers to be what they are, and then, if he so desires, defend the expediency in particular circumstances of allowing them the right to be what they are. He must speak as one of *us*, defending *their* liberties. To the extent he insists that they are on our side, that we can defend our liberties only by uncritically defending theirs, he will be taken as speaking as one of them.

Alan F. Westin: OUR FREEDOM—AND THE RIGHTS OF COMMUNISTS—A REPLY TO IRVING KRISTOL

Once, so a Spanish legend tells us, there grew in the forest a vine so strong that no animal could break it. Contests were held among the beasts, at which a piece of the vine would be cut and tied to a massive boulder so that champions from far and wide could pit their strength against it. Time after time the cords remained unbroken. One day, after the elephant had tugged in vain and the animals stood marveling at the vine's strength, a fox slipped over to it and, unnoticed, gnawed away at the strands. Ignoring the jeers of the spectators, he then walked over to the end of the rope, gave one firm pull, and the vine broke at the gnawed section. Thus, we are told, a fox succeeded where the mammoth beasts of the forest had failed.

In recent months, the problem of redefining our constitutional freedoms in a cold-war setting has received public attention, much of it stimulated by an article by Irving Kristol in the March issue of *Commentary*. So brilliantly does this article read that it has won acclaim from John Haynes Holmes, Ernest Angell, Norman Thomas, Ludwig Lewisohn, Paul Hays, and many other diverse liberals, while labor unions, private organizations, and the Mutual Security Agency have

reprinted its contents. Yet, as one rereads it, there emerges a feeling of having witnessed a dangerous gnawing away of strands, in the form of exceptions, from the vine of civil freedoms, a process which—without the elephantine strainings of McCarthyism—may still jeopardize the rope itself.

The central question of Mr. Kristol's article is posed by its subtitle, "Do We Defend Our Rights by Protecting Communists?" and the answer given is a resounding "No!"—expanded to include fellow-travelers as well. Stripped to essentials, the argument is as follows: The situation regarding civil liberties is confused today because certain duped liberals are defending Communists and Communist fellow-travelers when the issues at stake are not civil liberties at all but simply questions of "Communism." Such behavior brands liberals as pro-Communist before the American people and accounts for Senator McCarthy's victories over liberals in the battle for civil liberties. The solution to this confusion, it is argued, is to redefine the battle lines. The liberal must establish his anti-Communism in a particular way outlined by Mr. Kristol. Then, *if* he should desire to do so, the liberal can employ a "sober"

Reprinted with permission from *Commentary*, XIV (July 1955), pp. 33-40. Copyright 1955, American Jewish Committee.

approach and defend the civil rights of Communists and fellow-travelers as a tactic of "expediency in particular circumstances."

Now, I would agree wholeheartedly with Mr. Kristol that Communists pose a problem for American society, that there is an unbridgeable gulf between the Communist and the liberal, and that not every time the activities of Communists are restricted is an issue of civil liberties raised. I would further agree that in the past there have been "defenses" of civil liberties that were, in reality, propaganda operations by persons who do not believe in our concepts of civil liberties, and that in such campaigns the liberal must take no part. Lastly, I would agree that the liberal must defend civil liberties as a liberal, or as Mr. Kristol puts it, "as one of *us*, defending *their* liberties."

But although these important observations are found in Mr. Kristol's article, they are the shrubbery and not the real roots of his argument. These roots are to be found in four important premises on which he rests his case.

First, Mr. Kristol establishes strikingly narrow standards of anti-Communism, yet postulates these particular standards as absolute essentials for the liberal who would defend civil liberties. We are told that the American people "know" that Senator McCarthy is, "like them, unequivocally anti-Communist," and repeatedly throughout the article Senator McCarthy's peculiar brand of anti-Communism is equated with the national will. But even recognizing the Senator's appeal to large segments of the population, such a unitary concept of anti-Communism is as dubious factually as it is a dangerous perspective for examining civil liberties. There is, after all, a vital difference between the political

opportunism and special pleading of Senator McCarthy and the anti-Communism of social democracy, which adds to the exposure of Stalinists the necessity for support of economic and military aid bills to halt Communism abroad, and a loyalty to constitutional freedoms at home. To accept the McCarthy index on behalf of the nation concedes without justification one flank of the civil liberties battle line.

Again, in his standards of anti-Communism, Mr. Kristol transforms personal conceptions of history into categorical imperatives for every liberal who would defend civil liberties. Thus we are told that the liberal can establish his anti-Communism only by confessing the liberal "sins," chiefly that the New Deal "lent aid and comfort to Stalinist tyranny." With a remarkable "facility for nose-counting," as Joseph Rauh termed it, Mr. Kristol explains that the "major segment of American liberalism" during the New Deal were simply parrots of the Communist line who denied the existence of Soviet concentration camps, "approved" the purge trials, "applauded" the massacre of the non-Communists in Spain by the GPU during the Civil War, and gave "its blessing" to the liquidation of millions of Soviet kulaks. Because of this past, only a public breast-beating for these errors will prove the liberal an anti-Communist today.

Mr. Kristol has, of course, every right to his own reading of American liberalism during the period of the New Deal. But to say that agreement with this controversial and monolithic portrait of New Deal liberals is the requirement for one's public acceptance as an anti-Communist, is simply an attempt to impose a partisan perspective under the guise of helping the campaign for civil liberties. Just as liberals do not accept

Senator McCarthy as the index of anti-Communism, neither will they accept Mr. Kristol's stained canvas of New Deal liberalism as the *sine qua non* for an "unconfused" civil liberties struggle.

The second premise of Mr. Kristol's analysis is his repudiation of the distinction between legitimate civil freedoms of Communists and the commission by them of conspiratorial or criminal acts that threaten our free institutions. The danger to American society from a Communist's being treated with procedural fairness before the McCarran Committee is blended with the danger caused by Communists working at the top level of the Atomic Energy Commission. Both sets of activity are placed beyond the pale of civil freedoms.

This merging of civil liberties situations into simple matters of Communism assumes bizarre proportions when applied factually. The Hollywood Ten hearings before the House Committee on Un-American Activities involved for Mr. Kristol solely the right of Communists and fellow-travelers to make movies at plush salaries. There were no issues here of the right to counsel; to be confronted by, reply to, and cross-examine your accusers; to exercise the Fifth Amendment's guarantee against compulsory self-incrimination or to delimit the scope of questioning into a person's social and political affiliation by a committee of Congress. The University of California faculty oath, in Mr. Kristol's eyes, was merely a case of a university establishing a justified policy of not hiring Communists and fellow-travelers. Only through "undue hysteria" could one find a duty to speak up against the imposition of a test oath in violation of the California constitution (as the California court itself declared), or against

the implications of such administrative procedures applied to university life in a free society. In similar fashion, Mr. Kristol excludes from the range of civil liberties the Congressional examination of Owen Lattimore, since this was merely exposing an enormously effective Communist-liner who shaped our China policy. To view this as a matter of protecting "dissent" or "nonconformity" is labeled ridiculous.

From these illustrations, it becomes clear that Mr. Kristol, despite two hurried genuflections to "free speech" and "equal rights," possesses a remarkably dehydrated conception of a civil liberties issue. That he invokes the errors and dangers of Communism to justify this, shows how far his position is removed from the essence of constitutional guarantees. These have always rested on the notion that exceptions are permitted only when absolutely necessary for the preservation of our basic values. A sense of proportion must attend the recognition of dangers to our society from native Communism. To suggest that procedural fairness and the rights established by the First Amendment imperil our liberty bears an unfortunate resemblance to the philosophy of Military Judge Effingham Swan in Sinclair Lewis's novel *It Can't Happen Here,* who began a "hearing" on subversive activities with the statement: "*Habeas corpus*—due processes of law—too, too bad!—All those ancient sanctities, dating, no doubt, from Magna Carta—been suspended—oh, just temporarily, y'know—state of crisis—unfortunate necessity. . . ."

The third basis for Mr. Kristol's analysis is his portrait of the men who today defend the civil liberties of Communists and fellow-travelers: ". . . the Alan Barths, the Henry Steele Commagers, the Zechariah Chafees, the Howard Mumford Joneses, the Ralph Barton Perrys, the William O. Douglases." These men, and civil libertarians in general, are pictured as believing: (a) that Communists are merely a more radical or fanatic brand of liberal; (b) that Communists are "on our side" in the battle for civil liberties; and (c) that the fate of Communist *ideas* involves the fate of liberalism in America. This is a very handy whipping boy to bang around for nine double-column pages but it is representative of organized liberalism only in Mr. Kristol's imagination. True, there are many such persons as Mr. Kristol describes. But only by sidestepping the essential and dominant position of the quoted writers, and by totally ignoring the active anti-Communism of such liberal organizations as the Americans for Democratic Action and the American Civil Liberties Union can Mr. Kristol's villain be equated with the liberals who today defend the civil liberties of Communists.

In judging the accuracy of this picture, one should also observe that not only the intellectual conclusions of these men are challenged but that their very honesty is cleverly put into issue. Professor Commager, we are told, deludes us with "slight of hand"; Alan Barth employs a "liberal rhetoric of insinuation"; and Francis Biddle composed his book *The Fear of Freedom* out of a "sense of shame and a cowardliness to confess that shame." This whole school of liberals is then adroitly stripped of their anti-Communist beliefs, for Mr. Kristol declares that they are men who view Communism "out of the left corner of the eye," and that their rejection of Communism is only a "repudiation aiming to linger in the memory as a floating credential."

This is fine phrase-making, but it is at the same time literary tar-and-feathering, ruthless and unjustified. A smear is still a smear, even when done in onomatopoeia. One questions seriously whether such an approach helps end "confusion" or provides a guide to action for persons genuinely concerned with civil freedoms.

Fourth, there is a constant note running through Mr. Kristol's article which suggests that maybe liberals need not protect the principles of civil liberties at all when Communists or fellow-travelers are involved, even after the "confusion" has been cleared away. For Mr. Kristol keynotes his argument by stating: "*If* a liberal wishes to defend the civil liberties of Communists and Communist fellow-travelers. . . ." and "*If* he so desires [the liberal can] defend the expediency in particular circumstances of allowing them the right to be what they are." Here, the preservation of civil freedoms receives the emotional importance of choosing between a blue or a green toothbrush. The liberal himself seems to have no stake in it; American society seems to be without concern in the outcome. After the violence of Mr. Kristol's attack on the "confusion" of civil liberties today, we should mark well the serenity he attains once a cataloguing of sins, omissions, and deceptions has been completed.

Having identified the four pillars on which this article rests, we can recognize the structure for what it really is. Mr. Kristol has not selected among alternative courses of action in the struggle to preserve civil liberties. He has not resolved "confusion." He has not created a new, more honest, more realistic method for engaging in civil liberties campaigns. He has simply redefined the term "civil liberties" to remove the necessity of having to participate in the actual, important cases of civil liberties that are current today. He would remain uncommitted until there is a really clear case of procedural unfairness, not this shilly-shally over Owen Lattimore, the Hollywood Ten, and the Joint Anti-Fascist Refugee Committee. He would remain inactive until there is a real purge of a university, not this halfway business out at the University of California. He requires impeccable, unblemished victims of McCarthyism, not these ambiguous characters like Oliver Edmund Clubb, John Stewart Service, and Philip Jessup. Mr. Kristol has, in brief, so effectively side-stepped the problem of civil liberties that he is standing forty yards to the rear, throwing rocks at the foibles of the participants.

The most effective way to demonstrate the inadequacy of this gloss on civil liberties is to restate the bedrock principles upon which our constitutional freedoms rest. Louis Waldman has done this eloquently in a speech presenting the New York State Bar Association's proposed code of procedure for Congressional hearings: "There are not two Bills of Rights, one for sinners and a different one for saints. From the standpoint of civil rights there are no such people as racketeers and non-racketeers, Communists and anti-Communists. There are only human beings with rights, privileges, and immunities guaranteed to them by the Constitution."

If this egalitarian rationale were the *only* reason for civil liberties, few persons would be fighting for their retention today, and it would be next to impossible to protect the civil rights of any nonconformists, let alone those of the Communist. In fact, however, there are at least three further, *"selfish"* concepts behind civil liberties, concepts that were recognized by the Minute Men and yet are still grade-A merchandise for the atomic age. It is these which provide the mass appeal for the civil libertarian, and, in the long sweep of American history, have triumphed over the McCarthys of each era.

First, one defends the civil liberties of Communists because under our system of constitutional precedents a loss of liberty by one defendant is a loss to each citizen who may attempt to claim the same right at a future date. The whole tapestry of our most precious civil freedoms is recorded in cases involving —not immaculates—but thieves, smugglers, murderers, religious fanatics, subversives, espionage agents, and sundry unsavory criminals. The right to criticize or defend civil liberty itself can be said to rest on the fact that an anti-Semitic publisher who printed a mess of filth denouncing Jewish "gangsters" was protected in the courts by our guarantee of a free press. When the Supreme Court first considered the question of government wire-tapping in 1928, the defendant was a smuggler who shipped two million dollars' worth of whiskey into the United States each year from Canada. The rights of free speech were reaffirmed in a case involving Father Terminiello, a leader of the racist Union of Christian Crusaders, who delivered an inflammatory speech in Chicago denouncing Jews and Negroes. Our security from unreasonable searches and seizures was recently put at stake when a grubby counterfeiter of ration coupons had his office raided by the police without a warrant.

Thus, the rights of John Howard Lawson, Harold Christoffel, Frederick Vanderbilt Field, and the Joint Anti-Fascists cannot be brushed aside as "underground conspiracy" and unrelated to "dissent" or "free thought." The consideration by the courts of federal loyalty programs, of guilt by association, of Feinberg Laws and McCarran Acts and Smith Acts, does not involve merely the interests of Communists and fellow-travelers. It intimately affects the interests of all persons who could be reached by such legislative and administrative measures, and in this day of tension the potential bite of these weapons is deep and wide.

True, as Mr. Kristol points out, this is a grueling job. True, the men of good will often wind up with their protests in the anthologies while the restrictions go merrily on. But the struggle to convince the masses of the American people to safeguard civil liberties has always been a minority battle. Professor Commager reminds us that "each generation has to vindicate these freedoms anew, and for itself." It may be difficult, in this era of Koreas, to reaffirm that the civil liberties of anti-Communists are bound up in the manner with which we deal with William Z. Foster, Gus Hall, Harry Bridges, and Edith Blau, but this is the cold fact.

Thus, the first reason why we defend the civil liberties of Communists is to protect ourselves—a homespun and uncomplicated reason that is as valid today as in 1735 when crusty old Andrew Hamilton traveled from Philadelphia to defend a New York printer of dubious taste named Peter Zenger accused of libeling the Royal Governor. Requiring one citizen to worry about restraints on government when the other fellow is in the jailhouse may be asking a good deal from our citizenry, but this is the basic assumption of our constitutional framework, and it has served us well for one hundred and sixty-three years.

The second reason why we defend the civil liberties of Communists is because of the concrete and harmful effects upon our society of failing to do

so. This "pragmatic necessity for freedom" has been capsuled by Professor Commager as follows: "It is, you see, with the practical consequences to our society of the limitations on freedom that we are concerned. We do not protect freedom in order to indulge error. We protect freedom in order to discover truth. We do not maintain freedom in order to permit eccentricity to flourish; we maintain freedom in order that society may benefit from criticism, even eccentric criticism. We do not encourage dissent for sentimental reasons; we encourage dissent because we cannot live without it."

With Professor Commager this is expressed in ringing prose. The subway rider echoes it when he nods securely to his neighbor, "Aw, let those birds talk, it's a free country, ain't it?" In both cases, this is the most hard-headed, dollars-and-cents reason for protecting complete civil liberties. The highly necessary loyalty program for scientists, designed to keep Communists out of atomic projects, may be so broadly framed and unwisely administered that we will lose the services of loyal scientists, jeopardize our atomic superiority, and harm the defense potential of the nation. Professor Walter Gellhorn of the Columbia Law School devotes his book *Security, Loyalty and Science* to establishing that this is taking place today, and urging that we drastically revise our federal loyalty program. Is it pro-Communist, soft, or looking out of the left corner of the eye to concern ourselves with the effect on our atomic program of loyalty procedures designed to deal with Communists?

Again, take the crisis in the foreign service caused by attacks upon Communists in the State Department and upon policy advisors such as Professor Lattimore. The Department cannot now obtain enough college graduates of top caliber to fill its needs, as Secretary of State Acheson explained, because of "the unwillingness of young men and women to subject themselves to that sort of attack." At the same time, experts of unimpeachable loyalty have declined to give advice to the State Department—when the Department plucks up courage enough to ask for it—even though these men are often the best informed in their field and their assistance vital for the formulation of an intelligent policy. Moreover, the *Foreign Service Journal* has reported a tendency by overseas personnel to hew to the official "line" in transmitting their reports, even though this "line" might contradict their on-the-spot judgment. The lessons of John Carter Vincent, Oliver Edmund Clubb, and John Stewart Service have done their work.

In this illustration of the effects of curtailing freedom—directed against Communists, of course—we see a threat to our foreign service. The fact that the goal involved was the important and necessary one of ridding our State Department of security risks is no solace for the atmosphere of fear which has developed. The end does not justify the means here any more than it did in the Soviet Union during the 1920's and 1930's, even though the Kristol school does not seem to recognize the parallel.

One more example of effects should be noted. Mr. Kristol states that it is absurd to view the University of California faculty oath controversy as a "purge." Only a few dozen out of over a thousand refused to sign, and after all, "one swallow does not make a spring, nor one injustice an apocalypse." Contrast this characterization with the *results* at California.

At the outset of the oath controversy, over three hundred faculty members met to declare their refusal to sign the oath. As pressures mounted and men were forced to choose between their principles and their livelihood, the number dropped. At the first sweep twenty-six "non-signers" were ejected for their refusal and thirty-seven others resigned from the university in explicit protest against the oath.

But the damage here cannot be measured numerically in faculty dismissals and resignations. What happened to the University of California as an institution when this cleansing of Communists took place? Fifty-five courses had to be dropped from the curriculum. The department of theoretical physics fell overnight from the best in the nation to a ghost unit—three-fourths of its internationally renowned scientists having left in protest. An institute under the department of psychology lost a contract with the Office of Naval Research because it no longer had sufficient personnel to meet navy standards. In the department of psychology itself, one thousand inquiries concerning graduate curriculum were received in the year before the oath controversy; only three hundred arrived the year following it. In less than a twelve-month period, more than forty-seven of the world's most distinguished scholars refused offers of appointment to the University of California. Students interviewed by the press replied that the whole year was a nightmare of suspicions, recriminations, and disrupted studies. The caucus replaced the seminar; the mass meeting dubbed for lectures. A great university, respected throughout the nation and the world for its faculty, its research projects, and its student life, was and is still disrupted ominously by a "justified" policy of the regents in removing "Communists and fellow-travelers" from their institution.

Thus, the second reason why we protect the civil liberties of Communists is because we want to keep our science developing at maximum efficiency, our foreign service ably staffed and advised, and our universities free of the tensions of an oath campaign. We defend the rights of Communists since, as the New York *Times* editorialized: "If, in the process of arming ourselves against Stalinist infiltration, we so modify our society that the same barriers to free thought or speech exist here as in the Soviet Union, then victory will be futile indeed."

The third basis for the civil libertarian's position is the need to preserve our moral leadership in the world as the arsenal of freedom. We are now a feared Goliath in a bipolar world, attempting to win as necessary allies the uncomfortable and distrustful nations of the Middle East, Asia, and Western Europe. So far, we have managed a successful policy of exports: guns, goods, and free institutions. But if we make unrequired exceptions here in the United States in the name of curbing Communism, our export of free institutions becomes that much cheaper, and Communist salesmanship about our capitalist police-state that much more alluring. Secretary of State Dean Acheson has warned, "Today we all represent the United States. . . . If there are acts or words of violence, discrimination, and irresponsibility, the world sees and hears them . . . for nations are continually watching."

The present situation with passports is a prime example. As signatory to the UN Universal Declaration on Human Rights, the United States pledged as "a common standard of achievement for all peoples and all nations" that "Everyone has the right to leave any country, including his own, and to return to his country" (Article 13, Paragraph 2). Citing this provision, we have repeatedly leveled official attacks at the refusal of totalitarian nations to permit their nationals to travel freely. Our protests have helped to demonstrate the nature of totalitarianism to our allies. Yet, in recent years, the Passport Division of the State Department has steadily increased its restrictions on the right of American citizens to travel abroad. Leo Isaacson was denied a passport to attend an international conference in Paris in 1948 since it favored the Greek guerrilla cause. Paul Robeson was refused permission to travel abroad to give concerts and make speeches. Dr. J. Henry Carpenter of the Protestant Council of New York was barred from visiting Japan for meetings with Japanese church leaders. Rockwell Kent, Dr. Edward Corson, Albert Kahn, Dr. Ralph Spitzer, Howard Fast, and Corliss Lamont have met similar refusals. United States immigration authorities prevented Vincent Hallinan, presidential candidate of the Progressive Party, from crossing the Canadian border to deliver a speech to a Vancouver labor union. There have been no hearings. There are no standards set for these refusals. In the few cases where the Passport Division has given an explanation, the sole ground asserted is that the trip would not be "in the best interests of the United States."

As could be expected, our departure from an observance of the right to free travel has already produced its effects abroad. State Department observers have reported a loss of American prestige in the capitals of Western Europe. The New York *Times* noted that "influential circles abroad . . . have begun to react cynically to United States pronouncements on intellectual freedom and exchange of persons, and are chiding this government for what they call 'hypocrisy' in this field." President Truman's 1951 call to the president of the Soviet Presidium for "communication . . . free and open, across international boundaries" has been undercut by our own passport practices.

It is no answer to this damaging situation to cite the dangers of Communist couriers to our national security and to argue that government officials must be given "the benefit of the doubt" in this area. Recognition of the courier threat is only the first level of analysis, and the appeal to trust government administrators is an undisguised retreat from analysis. Every citizen, after all, could be a Communist courier, especially since vital information would not likely be risked with a known Communist or a vocal fellow-traveler. In resolving this dilemma between security and individual liberty, a society under law must adopt fair and constitutional standards, and must provide its citizens an opportunity to be heard. As the editors of the *Yale Law Journal* wrote: "Under the circumstances of modern international life every American citizen has a constitutional right to a passport, and the protection of that right has become an urgent matter of national policy as well as of civil liberty. If our preaching [internationally] is to accord with our practice, that right should be curtailed only for good cause and with that regard for fairness embodied in the phrase 'due process.'"

If, instead, we continue to employ vague and undefined political criteria, at the discretion of administrators, without hearing or review, our prestige will continue to suffer. As Professor Elmer Graper observed in describing "American Influence on the Attitudes of Western Europe" (*The Annals of the American Academy of Political and Social*

Science, November 1951): ". . . the blatant accusations against public officials, the demagogic rantings and posturings . . . these and similar excesses tend to arouse doubts about our political maturity and uncertainty as to who really speaks for America. They even raise the question whether in our zeal to fight subversion at home we are not succeeding merely in imitating some of the worst features of Communism abroad. A democratic nation that expects others to follow it must present to the world an example of democracy in practice, a democracy which not only advocates the doctrine of human rights and individual liberty but also lives up to that doctrine."

In the tent show of the cold war, we have a top-notch medicine wagon, a booming set of drums, and our patent remedy for the world's ills is labeled "Uncle Samuel's Democracy." If we adulterate our product in the factory, however, we can expect to lose customers to another drummer even though he may be a complete charlatan.

Having outlined these three bases for the belief that we *do* defend our rights by protecting Communists, there remains the important inquiry into method. Clearly, when the liberal defends Communists, he must make an unequivocal distinction between the civil liberty involved and the individual or group concerned. He *must* defend the civil liberties of Eugene Dennis, but he need not take out a party card and condemn United Nations "germ warfare" to do so. Despite inferences to the contrary, most liberal organizations make exactly this distinction today. Briefs filed in the Supreme Court by such groups as the National Association for the Advancement of Colored People or the American Jewish Congress in cases involving the Communist party invariably begin with a clear statement explaining the interest the particular organization has, as liberal and anti-Communist, in preserving rights in the case at bar. When Senators begin using a Congressional committee as a personal bludgeon, liberals should attack this procedure whether Adrian Scott, Howard Fast, or Newbold Morris is under the klieg lights. But again, this is done through liberal organizations, as liberals, not through the Civil Rights Congress or a dummy "defense committee."

In his methods, the liberal must constantly apply the distinction between civil freedoms and anti-social acts. This is unquestionably a difficult task to perform in an age which demands solutions, not distinctions. But we cannot stop trying because of defeats, since despair will only allow broader violations of civil freedoms to develop in the vacuum of our fatigue. With "starch in our backbones," as Professor Edmund Cahn put it, we must stop the bullying of free America by waging *our* fight for the legitimate rights of every citizen. We must defend free speech for Communists: their right to call us "lackeys of imperialism" and "social fascists"; to picket the White House for aggression in Korea; to denounce the North Atlantic Treaty as Wall Street brokerage; and to preach that the Soviet Union is the land of economic milk and political honey. We must rip off the Paper Curtain which prevents citizens from traveling abroad, even though they may present views of America which will "embarrass" us at home. We must keep the soapbox and printing presses accessible; the ballot booth and meeting hall unlocked. But we do not have to allow theft of atomic secrets or acts of sabotage in industry, or need to ignore the political affiliations of those who staff our Central Intelligence Agency. This line of demarcation is the basis of the civil libertarian's position: when he succeeds in conveying its vitalness to the American people, he will have won the battle for civil liberties.

From our constitutional heritage, our social progress, and our responsibilities of international leadership comes the answer to Mr. Kristol's question—we defend the civil liberties of Communists to preserve our own rights and to advance the national welfare. Our civil freedoms in 1952 will remain "unconfused" as long as we recognize that, despite inflation, eternal vigilance is *still* the price of liberty.

✓ Sidney Hook: REFLECTIONS ON THE SMITH ACT

Strongly influenced by the instrumentalist philosophy of John Dewey and eloquently committed to the tradition of democratic socialism, Sidney Hook has established a reputation for philosophical inquiry and for polemical involvement in radical politics and journalism. His reflections on the Smith Act, like Kristol's on the more general problems raised by the Communist Party, brought forth numerous responses from other parties to the controversy.

THE Smith Act makes it unlawful for any person to advocate the overthrow of the government by force and violence (Section Two) or for any person to attempt to commit or to conspire to commit such advocacy (Section Three).

This Act and the various judicial opinions on its constitutionality are among the most discussed, and the most unread, of modern official documents. In any such discussion, several sorts of issues must be distinguished. One is the constitutionality of the Act. A second is its wisdom. A third is the justice of its application to the Communist Party. Another way of putting this may focalize the moot points better. Is the law behind the indictment of the leaders of the Communist Party constitutional? Constitutional or not, is it wise to have brought the charge? Were the defendants, i.e., the leaders of the Communist Party, guilty of the charge— do they actually advocate the use of "force and violence"?

The constitutionality of the Smith Act, it may be argued, is a matter of history since in fact the Supreme Court has decided the question. However, no adjudication of any Congressional legislation as constitutional can be regarded as final; the Supreme Court can always reverse itself by adopting the fiction that a new case before it, apparently involving the very same issues on which it has

taken a stand, is in some respects relevantly different, and therefore provides the ground for a new decision. Both cases then become precedents to be cited by the Court on subsequent occasions for whichever decision it sees fit to make.

But most discussion about whether a piece of legislation is constitutional or not actually is a discussion about whether it is wise or not, "democratic" or not, enlightened or not. Anyone who reflects upon the number and variety of laws declared constitutional in the past, some of which supported the institution of slavery, will admit at once that an act may be constitutional and unwise, and, like the Federal Income Tax when it was first adopted, wise and unconstitutional. I shall therefore be more concerned with the wisdom of this act than with its constitutionality.

There is one preliminary question which must be cleared up concerning "the right to revolution," since it has been asserted that the Smith Act abrogates this right. Reference is made to this right, not in the Constitution, but in the Declaration of Independence, where it does not appear as an absolute right but as one justified under certain conditions. Only when life, liberty and the pursuit of happiness are threatened with destruction do "the people" have a right

Reprinted with the author's permission from *Heresy, Yes—Conspiracy, No* (New York: John Day, 1953), pp. 94-119.

to overthrow their rulers. The Declaration distinguishes between revolutions of this character and "insurrections" of minorities which the English king is accused of fomenting among the American colonists.

Some writers have inferred that because there is a justification for revolution in situations in which democratic processes are absent, a similar justification therefore exists in situations in which these processes are the rule. This overlooks the various connotations of the term "right." The term "right" may be used in the legal sense and the moral sense. Legally, a right is any claim to goods or services or privileges, made by one or more individuals, and which society stands ready to enforce. Legally, therefore, it is utter nonsense to speak of the right to revolution. Justice Hand disposes effectively of the claim that there is a *legal* right to advocate violence when he says, in his opinion for the Court of Appeals which found the Smith Act constitutional:

The advocacy of violence may, or may not, fail: but in neither case can there be any "right" to use it. Revolutions are often "right"; but a "right of revolution" is a contradiction in terms, for a society which acknowledged it, could not stop at tolerating conspiracies to overthrow it, but must include their execution.

However, in all historical situations, whether democratic or not, individuals have a moral right to revolution in the sense that, if they are rationally convinced that their fundamental values can be preserved only by the overthrow of the existing regime, they are morally justified in making the attempt. Believing what they do, it may even be their duty to make the attempt. But by the same token, individuals who are rationally convinced that any attempt to over-

throw the existing regime by force and violence will destroy their fundamental values, will have a moral right to suppress the revolutionists.

This does not mean that in any particular historical situation both sides are equally justified in their analysis of the values involved and of the needs and interests in which values are rooted. One or another side may be hasty, partial, or mistaken. So long as the processes of reflective inquiry are kept open, what appear to be ultimate and inarbitrable conflicts of interest may prove to be negotiable. When such conflicts are not negotiable, what is shown is not that moral values have no objective reality but that they are not universal.

There is nothing self-contradictory in asserting that, in *any* society, human beings have a moral right or rational claim to revolution. What *is* self-contradictory is the belief, by someone who regards himself as a principled democrat, in the right to revolution in a democratic society. Societies whose democratic processes operate unabridged and whose decisions truly rest upon the freely given consent of a majority, may act in such a way as to cause moral men to use revolutionary means to overthrow them. But when men act in this manner, they cannot sincerely or consistently call themselves democrats, even when they consider themselves God's angry men. Democratic government and good government are not identical in meaning. That democratic government is more likely to produce good government than non-democratic government is only an empirical hypothesis, warranted by most of the historical evidence but not by all of it.

These considerations may appear to be abstract, but failure to think them through almost invariably leads to confusion. To one who accepts the principles and institutional practices that define a democracy, there is neither a moral nor a legal right to use force and violence to overthrow a democracy which satisfies the definition, merely because its fruits are personally unsatisfactory. On the other hand, while he may not have a legal right to overthrow a dictatorship, because it writes the rules of law, he certainly has a moral right to do so, because by his action he is passing judgment on the existing rules of law.

On the assumption that they are sincerely convinced of the badness of democracy, we may grant to the Hitlers and Stalins, and to other totalitarians of the more reasonable Platonic brood, the "moral" right to revolt against a democracy, provided we understand that as democrats we have the "moral" right—nay, duty—to crush them, when and if they make the attempt, or prepare for that attempt. Any criticism of the Smith Act as undemocratic by totalitarians, especially of the Communist and Fascist stripe, we can dismiss as a piece of indecent hypocrisy.

My concern is with the Smith Act from the point of view of a believer in democracy. All such believers would admit that legislation which punishes the overt act of revolt or insurrection should be enacted and enforced. But the Smith Act makes punishable, not the overt actions, which are covered by other legislation, but the advocacy of, or incitement to, the use of force or violence. Further, it makes punishable a conspiracy to teach any doctrine containing such advocacy or incitement.

What is a "conspiracy"? Some clarification is necessary at this point. In many contexts, the word "conspiracy" refers to non-verbal overt behavior. As usually employed outside of legal contexts, it designates active planning with others and involves something more than the use of words. The verb "to conspire," however, has a much more comprehensive meaning. It denotes, not merely the overt act of conspiracy, but the process of conspiring. On occasions, the use of speech, oral and written, between two or more persons may be considered as part of the process of conspiring—depending on the place, the circumstances, and the nature of the words used.

Many people who are critical of the Smith Act concentrate their fire against section three which makes it illegal "to conspire" to advocate the use of force and violence. Since there was no evidence indicated of "conspiracy," in the usual sense of overt non-verbal behavior —say accumulation of arms—they conclude that it is absurd to have charged the Communist defendants with having attempted "to conspire." This criticism is based on the assumption that the use of words by themselves can never be evidence of an attempt "to conspire."

It is the great merit of Justice Jackson's opinion to call attention to the legal fact that in our system of law conspiracies are adjudged to exist on the basis of the same *kind* of evidence that was introduced in the case of the Communist Party leaders. The legal rule concerning conspiracy in interstate commerce, for example, and the admissibility of evidence chiefly of a verbal kind in establishing the existence of such conspiracy, has never been challenged by the opponents of the Smith Act.

"Conspiracies of labor-unions, trade associations, and news agencies," writes Justice Jackson in his concurring opinion on the Smith Act, "have been condemned although accomplished, evidenced, and carried out, like the conspiracy here, chiefly by letter-writing, meetings, speeches, and organizations." He goes on to cite from an opinion of Justice Holmes involving the Sherman Anti-Trust Act: "Coming next to the objection that no overt act is laid, the answer is that the Sherman Act punishes the conspiracies at which it is aimed on the common law footing,—that is to say, it does not make the doing of any act other than the act of conspiring, a condition of liability." To which Justice Jackson adds the dry observation: "It is not to be supposed that the power of Congress to protect the nation's existence is more limited than its power to protest interstate commerce."

Consequently, there is a legal warrant to accept as evidence of conspiracy to do something unlawful, speech, writing and organizational activity. The main question, then, is not Section Three of the Smith Act, which forbids conspiracy to do what is proscribed in Section Two, but Section Two itself, which forbids the advocacy of the overthrow of government by force or violence. If it is wrong to advocate the use of force and violence, it is wrong to conspire to do so. But is it wrong to advocate the use of force and violence?

Since the First Amendment enjoins Congress from passing any laws abridging freedom of speech, some opponents of the Smith Act regard it as unconstitutional on this ground. But, if the first amendment were construed literally, this would make even laws against criminal libel unconstitutional. Whoever reads the First Amendment as if it made the right to speech absolute and unconditioned would find himself committed to the same kind of absurdities as anyone who took the statement in the Declaration of Independence about all men being created free and equal as a proposition in theology or biology instead of political ethics.

Outside of legal circles, this appeal to the right of free speech as an absolute is so common and is buttressed so often by invoking mistakenly the position of Justices Holmes and Brandeis, that it is pertinent here to quote from an opinion of Justice Holmes speaking for a unanimous court:

The First Amendment while prohibiting legislation against free speech as such cannot have been, and obviously was not, intended to give immunity for every possible use of language. . . . We venture to believe that neither Hamilton nor Madison, nor any other competent person then or later, ever supposed that to make criminal the counselling of a murder within the jurisdiction of Congress would be an unconstitutional interference with free speech.

If a democracy does not accept the beliefs in absolute rights, how does it morally distinguish itself from a dictatorship? I shall consider this question later; but for the moment I wish to point out that the defendants tried under the Smith Act did not fall back upon any assertion of the absolute right of freedom of advocacy. Their main contention was that, even if the charge were true, such advocacy did not constitute a "clear and present" danger of the violent overthrow of the government.

This in principle recognizes what common sense has always acknowledged, *viz.*, that if an act is criminal or immoral, it is wrong to advocate or counsel its commission even if the liability for such advocacy is not enforced. I cannot resist quoting from an earlier opinion of Justice Hand a generation ago which expresses with felicity the logic, the ethics, and the psychology of the matter:

One may not counsel or advise others to

violate the law as it stands. Words are not only the keys of persuasion, but the triggers of action, and those which have no purport but to counsel the violation of law cannot by any latitude of interpretation be a part of that public opinion which is the final source of government in a democratic state.

The general principle which limits the right to free speech is not expressed in the Constitution but in a famous decision written by Justice Holmes, in which he stated that "the question in every case is whether the words are used in such circumstances and are of such a nature as to create a clear and present danger that will bring about the substantive evils that Congress has a right to prevent."

Like the phrase "due process of law," the phrase "clear and present" danger seems to have a fluid meaning. How clear must the danger be? To whom must the danger be clear? How present —today, this year, or the current century? And how great the danger? The Justices of the present court are at loggerheads with each other as to the exact meaning to give the phrase. Most discussions are frankly concerned more with what the words *should* mean, i.e., how they should be interpreted in specific cases, than with what they *did* mean to Holmes and Brandeis. What is true of constitutional interpretation generally is true of interpretations of dicta like "clear and present danger"—what seems reasonable to the Court at any given time is read back into the original intent of Holmes' words.

If we examine the context in which Holmes first used the phrase, we may be able to get a better notion of what he had in mind, independently of whether we desire to accept or reject his proposed criterion. In the Schenk case the defendant was charged with obstructing recruiting, and causing military insubordination by denouncing conscription. The most inciting sentence of the handbill, only a few of which were circulated, was, according to Justice Vincent, the following: "You must do your share to maintain, support and uphold the rights of the people of this country."

It was this action—the distribution of a handbill with such a mild incitement —which Holmes, speaking for a unanimous court, held a "clear and present danger" of imperiling the conscription program and causing military insubordination. It follows at once that Holmes could not have meant by his criterion an action that threatened to be successful. No one in his most fantastic dream could imagine that the circulation of a few leaflets by a lone individual would successfully undermine the American program of conscription. Nonetheless, Justice Douglas in his minority opinion on the Smith Act denies that "a clear and present danger" of revolutionary overthrow exists on the ground that the Communist petitioners have not "the slightest chance of achieving their aims."

Now it so happens, although Justice Douglas is unaware of it, that the Kremlin often instructs its fifth columns to make a bid for the conquest of political power by force and violence even when the probability of success is extremely small, and even when the direst predictions of failure have been made by those ordered to seize power. The reasons for this need not now concern us: they flow from strategic considerations in the Kremlin's plans for world domination. In the 1920's such futile insurrections took place in Thuringia, Hamburg, and Canton. Even a wildly improbable effort at overthrow, one foredoomed to failure, may have very grave consequences for the community. Whatever the "clear and present danger" formula may mean, to any reasonable person it cannot mean that speech advocating a crime should be curbed only when it is extremely probable that the crime will be successful.

What is relevant in determining whether or not to invoke the clear and present danger formula, is the probability of *an attempt being made*, not the probability of the attempt succeeding. The probability that an attempt will actually be made to carry out what is advocated, is a function of two things: the readiness of those advocating revolutionary overthrow to act when they believe the situation is ripe—something which the jury is called on to decide—and, second, the political state of the world, the temper of the times, the objective threats to the existence of democratic institutions—which the court pronounces on (for no good reason that I can see, since this is not a matter of law but of fact).

The majority opinion interprets the phrase in the same way as Judge Learned Hand does: "In each case (courts) must ask whether the gravity of the 'evil,' discounted by its improbability, justifies such invasion of free speech as is necessary to avoid the danger." The term "evil" refers to the substantive evils Congress has a right to prevent, and the term "improbability" is used synonymously here with "remoteness." How remote is the danger of the Communist conspiracy making some attempt to carry out what it advocates?

All the opinions in the Smith Act, except for the dissents of Justices Black and Douglas, recognize that the phrase "clear and present danger" is no shibboleth, and that in every case its intelli-

gent use requires an analysis of the particular situation. Some consistency there must be, however, if these words are not to become entirely arbitrary. What seems extremely puzzling to me is how anyone can approve of the determination that a clear and present danger existed in the Schenk case—when Justice Holmes first formulated his principle—and contest the finding that a clear and present danger exists in the case of Dennis *et al.*, who are an integral part of a highly organized international conspiracy. For my own part, it seems to me that the Supreme Court was clearly unjustified in its decision in the Schenk case. The whole incident was trivial, and there was not the remotest chance that Schenk could have had any influence on the American conscription program. I do not believe it can fairly be construed even as an attempt to obstruct that program.

To approve of the decision in the Schenk case and disapprove of it in the Dennis case, as so many liberals have done, makes no sense at all. This is all the truer because instead of referring the Schenk case back for retrial so that the *jury* could determine the *facts* about the clear and present danger, the Court made such determination itself. Justices Black and Douglas who believe that the jury should have passed on this point in the case of Dennis *et al.* do not criticize either the decision or procedure in the Schenk case. So far as I know Norman Thomas was the only outstanding liberal figure who, although approving of "the clear and present danger" interpretation, emphatically criticized the Court in the Schenk case both for taking jurisdiction to determine the facts and for its decision on the facts.

As the Smith Act has now been interpreted by the courts, it applies only to cases in which a "clear and present" danger exists that an attempt at revolutionary overthrow will be made. Now the question arises: who is to be the judge of whether or not a clear and present danger exists? Two different things have been confused in the court opinions on this question. The first question is whether or not the gravity and dangers of the times justifies, in the interest of national security, restrictions on the freedom of speech to advocate revolutionary overthrow. The second question is whether or not the specific case at bar, in which the defendants have been charged with conspiracy to advocate revolutionary overthrow, is one in which a clear and present danger flows from *this particular advocacy*. The opinion of the majority of the judges is that both of these questions are questions for the Court to decide. My own view is that the first question is one for Congress to decide since it involves a conflict of social interests—the interest in national security and the interest in free speech. The second question is one for the jury to decide. I shall discuss these two questions separately.

The first question, as Justice Frankfurter points out in his remarkable concurring opinion, is one which obviously falls within the legislative power. It is a matter of policy. And responsibility for policy rests with the elected representatives who may be refused our confidence at election time, and not with judges who are beyond reach. As far as policy goes, a judge's vote counts for one and no more than one, and is cast like every other citizen's vote. Justice Frankfurter's words in this connection ought to be inscribed in letters of gold on the portals of the Supreme Court. "Our duty to abstain from confounding policy with constitutionality demands perceptive humility as well as self-restraint in not declaring unconstitutional what in a judge's private judgment is unwise and even dangerous."

Leaving aside now the question of constitutionality, was Congress justified in assuming that there exists a clear and present danger of sufficient gravity to warrant restriction on advocacy of revolutionary overthrow? That a danger to our national survival exists which is clear, present, flourishing, and extremely powerful, seems to me to be undeniable to any sober view. This danger flows from the unremitting crusade of the Kremlin, now using open violence, now subversion and espionage, against the United States. These dangers may be *distinguished* in their internal and external aspects, but they cannot be *separated*. It is communism as an international movement whose capital is Moscow which is the enemy of American democracy; and the American Communist Party, no matter what its size or influence (which is not entirely inconsiderable), is an integral part of that movement. Whoever overlooks this has overlooked the main point. For without this organic tie to the Soviet state apparatus with all its engines of war, espionage and terror, the American Communist Party would have only nuisance value, its members would be ineffectual, candidates for the political psychopathic ward now inhabited by various other Communist splinter groups like the Trotskyites. It is not the speech of members of the Communist Party which makes them dangerous but their organizational ties, for this in effect makes them a para-military fifth column of a powerful state, ready to strike whenever their foreign masters give the word.

The aim of the Smith Act was certainly justified in the light of the available facts. But the method of achieving this aim—making powerless the Soviet fifth column—was inept. The proscription should have been placed, not on speech to achieve revolutionary overthrow, but on organization to achieve it, and not merely any organization but an organization set up and controlled by a foreign power.

I know a gentle, rather weak-headed old man, formerly a member of the I.W.W., who vehemently makes speeches advocating insurrection by the working classes outside the parliamentary process, and the destruction not only of the state, in which he professes not to believe, but of capitalists as a class. He sounds bloodthirsty, but anyone who hears him knows that it is all rheum and wind. Technically, however, according to the Smith Act, Section Two, Paragraph A, Subhead 1, this feeble, harmless old man would be liable to prosecution and punishment. Now, surely Congress did not intend this.

In 1940 the leaders of the Trotskyist Socialist Workers Party were found guilty of violating the Smith Act. I have always been mystified as to why the Supreme Court refused to pass on the constitutionality of the Smith Act in this case. Although like other Communists they denied it, this Trotskyist faction does believe in, and firmly advocates, the revolutionary overthrow of the American government by force or violence. It accepts the thesis and Resolutions of the first four Congresses of the Communist International, and if anything, is theoretically more intransigent than official Communists whom it has regarded, first as "centrists," and then as "thermidorians." It has all the venom of the Stalinists but not the fangs. Al-

though professing loyalty to the Soviet Union as a "worker's state"—one which would shoot them out of hand if it could reach them!—this group's advocacies and activities never constituted the slightest threat to the security or survival of the United States. The reason is that, although organized, they are completely independent of any foreign power, do not take orders from the Kremlin, and do not collaborate in the espionage activities of the Communist Party. Their prosecution was, not merely foolish, but scandalous, and was ordered by President Roosevelt in payment of a political debt to Daniel Tobin whose control of the Teamster's Union was being threatened by a Minneapolis local, controlled by Trotskyists. Certainly, Congress did not have such groups in mind when it passed the Smith Act. Yet they were liable under Section Two, Paragraph A, Subhead 3, which outlaws any organization which advocates revolutionary overthrow.

Judge Hand admits that the wording of the Act, literally construed, would "make criminal the fulminations of a half-crazy zealot on a soap-box, calling for an immediate march on Washington." As the Supreme Court has interpreted the Act, however, it has remedied the deficiency by in effect introducing "the clear and present danger" clause. Although Judge Hand is apparently dubious about the wisdom of revising the language of the Smith Act, it seems to me that it would be a marked step in clarification as well as an obstacle to arbitrary misinterpretation by a future court, were Congress to amend the Smith Act in order to insert the italicized words in the relevant sections as follows:

(A) It shall be unlawful for any person—
    (1) To knowingly or willfully advocate, abet, advise, or teach, *in the case*

that it constitutes a clear and present danger, the duty, necessity, desirability or propriety of overthrowing or destroying any government in the United States by force or violence. . . .

(3) To organize or help to organize, *in the case that it constitutes a clear and present danger,* any society, group, or assembly of persons who teach, advocate, or encourage the overthrow or destruction of any government in the United States by force and violence. . . .

A certain area of ambiguity will always remain, since what constitutes "a clear and present danger" will have to be determined in each case. But the explicit presence of such a phrase in the law itself would go a long way towards discouraging indiscriminate use of the Smith Act against private individuals sounding off on their own, and societies of crackpots and amateur conspirators who are greater threats to the peace of mind of their parents and wives than to the security of the nation. I believe this amendment desirable despite the fact that the widely heralded predictions, made with such hysterical fervor, that the Smith Act would be used against liberals, democrats, and socialists in an attempt to suppress thought have not materialized.

This brings me to the second question, referred to above, namely whether any particular advocacy of the use of revolutionary violence constitutes a clear and present danger. In the case of the Communist Party defendants, the jury was called upon to determine only whether they violated the statute but not whether such violation constituted a clear and present danger. That determination was made by Judge Medina as a matter of law, affirmed by Judge Hand, and upheld by Justice Vinson who wrote the majority opinion of the Supreme Court. Judge Medina in his instructions to the jury advised them as follows:

If you are satisfied that the evidence establishes beyond a reasonable doubt that the defendants, or any of them, are guilty of a violation of the statute, as I have interpreted it to you, I find it as a matter of law that there is a sufficient danger of a substantive evil that the Congress has a right to prevent, to justify the application of the statute under the first amendment of the Constitution.

This is a matter of law with which you have no concern. It is a finding on a matter of law which I deem essential to support my ruling that the case should be submitted to you to pass on the guilt or innocence of the defendants.

I agree with the finding but I cannot see in what way this is a matter of law. It seems to me that sufficient evidence was introduced, or could easily have been introduced, to convince any but Communists, their sympathizers, and doctrinaire pacifists who believe Stalin has a loving heart, that the international Communist movement, of which these defendants were trusted members, constitutes a clear and present threat to the preservation of free American institutions and our national independence. The only valid point Justice Douglas' dissent makes is that this question should have been considered by the jury since it is a question of fact. But whether Court or jury should pass on this question, Justice Douglas himself denies in the most emphatic way that the existence of the Communist movement creates any clear and present danger to the nation.

If this is a question of fact it is best answered by those who have some familiarity with the relevant fact—and on the question of the Communist movement Justice Douglas has given no evidence of special familiarity.

The late Justice Brandeis was supposed to have introduced a revolution in the approach of the Supreme Court by trying to dig out the empirical data bearing on the effects of social legislation like minimum wage laws, instead of trying to deduce wise policies from ambiguous legal expressions. Although the Justices of the Supreme Court in some recent cases have shown increasing awareness of some of the grosser historical facts about the Communist movement in modern times, on the whole they have been seriously remiss in acquainting themselves with the verifiable facts about Communist theory, practice, and organization. I do not know what judicial qualifications Justice Frank Murphy had for his elevation to the Supreme Court, but his decision in the Schneiderman case, in which he found that the Communist Party did not believe in what it expressly said it believed, betrays a sublime indifference to the easily verifiable truth. Although of late, and especially in considering the Smith Act, the Supreme Court Justices have shown a commendable spirit in repairing the gaps in their knowledge, even Justice Frankfurter, who has read belatedly, alas, the Canadian *Report of the Royal Commission to Investigate Communication of Secret and Confidential Information to Agents of a Foreign Power,* adds in a footnote to an opinion which otherwise ranks with the best of Holmes and Brandeis: "There appears to be little reliable evidence demonstrating directly that the Communist Party in this country has recruited persons willing to engage in espionage or other unlawful activity on behalf of the Soviet Union." Not only does sworn testimony and corroborative evidence exist, supplied by former secretaries of the Communist Party and by former active un-derground agents that the American Communist Party did recruit its members for espionage work and other unlawful activity; it is also part of the public record which individuals of the Central Committee were liaison officers with the three Soviet espionage organizations in this country, and were entrusted with the selection of personnel.

Justice Vinson offers a mild characterization of the nature of the Communist Party and of the historical situation in justification of the Court's finding of a clear and present danger. He says:

The formation by petitioners of such a highly organized conspiracy, with rigidly disciplined members subject to call when the leaders, these petitioners, felt that the time had come for action, coupled with the inflammable nature of world conditions, similar uprisings in other countries, and the touch-and-go nature of our relations with countries to whom petitioners were in the very least ideologically attuned, convince us that their convictions were justified on this score.

To this Justice Douglas acidly retorts: "That ruling is in my view not responsive to the issue in the case. We might as well say that the speech of petitioners is outlawed because Soviet Russia and her Red Army are a threat to peace." And why not? Under certain circumstances this might very well be the case. The elementary duty of the court, including Justice Douglas, is to study the techniques of infiltration, penetration, and open warfare waged by the Soviet Union and its agencies against the United States in Korea, Berlin, Western Europe, South and Central America, and Asia, and to assess the cumulative effects of its campaign of subversion and defamation. The members of the Communist Party are literally the fifth column of the Red Army, and the success and strategic position of that Army are certainly relevant in considering the danger, not merely of Communist advocacy, but of Communist organization in this country.

Justice Douglas does admit "that the nature of communism as a force on the world scene would, of course, be relevant to the issue of clear and present danger of petitioners' advocacy within the United States." But he makes no attempt to consider that nature. Instead he regards the political strength and position of the Communist Party in *this* country, ignoring its ties with the international Communist movement, as of "primary consideration," and scoffs at the notion that by their efforts, including their capacities for sabotage and espionage, they have even "the slightest chance of *achieving* their aims" (my italics). Of course, considered in isolation, the Communist Party has not the slightest chance of succeeding in its aims. But the point which Justice Douglas so elaborately misses is that they do *not* work in isolation but in a co-ordinated strategy which has behind it the power of a regime which controls the human and natural resources of a quarter of the world. Nor, as we have already seen, is the likelihood of the success of the conspiratorial action the decisive matter. An unsuccessful attempt can be productive of great misery. One plant needlessly struck, one atomic installation sabotaged, some key state secrets betrayed, in conjunction with the general strategy of the Soviet assault, may have effects out of all proportion to their apparent proximate causes. It is true that there are other laws besides the Smith Act which cover sabotage and espionage, but Justice Frankfurter is surely justified in calling attention to the fact that, according to the *Report* of the Royal Canadian Commission investigating the Communist espionage network, "conspiratorial characteristics of the Party similar to those shown in the evidence now before us were instrumental in developing the necessary motivation to cooperate in the espionage."

At the time Justice Douglas wrote his dissent, virtual war between one section of the Communist International and the United States as part of the U.N. was raging in Korea, the Communist war of nerves against the West was being thrown into high gear, neutralism was registering gains in Europe, and the shocking record of Communist espionage lay revealed, if only in part, before the world. To deny under these circumstances that an organization of some tens of thousands of conspirators, with a reliable periphery of some hundreds of thousands, constitutes a clear and present danger to the security of the nation is to manifest a stubborn will to believe that Providence or luck will protect those who are too blind to protect themselves.

That the Communist Party, despite its denials, actually advocates the use of force and violence is apparent from all its basic documents. The contention that the use of force and violence is reserved only to meet insurrectionary threats from non-Communists *after* Communists have peacefully and democratically come to power is disingenuous. A similar characterization must be made of the dodge adopted by John Strachey, when he was a Communist, in resisting the threat of deportation, needless at the time, by a nervous Attorney General. Communists, he said, do not advocate the use of violence; they merely predict it. But this runs counter to the entire Communist conception of the nature of a belief as a guide to action. Communists are safe in predicting the use of force and violence because in reality they advocate that use. Their very theory of knowledge instructs them that, in social affairs at least, all concepts are not merely predictive but directive.

The subterfuge that the use of force and violence is only a defensive measure, taken in advance against an anticipated reaction, is a contribution of Stalin to the ideological strategy of Bolshevism. Lenin and Trotsky were much more forthright on this score. In fact in the post-Leninist struggle for succession, Trotsky accused Stalin of lack of revolutionary integrity for not advocating insurrection as an offensive tactic in the conquering of state power. To which Stalin replied:

An original peculiarity of the revolutionary tactics of this period must be pointed out. This peculiarity consists therein that the revolution attempted to carry out every, or almost every step of its attack under the appearance of defense. There is no doubt that the refusal to permit the transfer of troops was a serious aggressive act of the revolution; nevertheless this attack was undertaken under the slogan of the defense of Petrograd against a possible attack of the external enemy. There is no doubt that the formation of the revolutionary committee was a still more serious attack against the Provisional Government; *nevertheless it was carried out under the slogan of the defense of the Petrograd Soviets against possible attacks of the counter-revolution.*
In *Errors of Trotskyism,* London, 1925, Eng. trans., pp. 225-226.

Communist Parties throughout the world have learned this lesson well. But they were not always so careful in the past as the following citation from William Z. Foster's *Towards Soviet America,* shows:

Even before the seizure of power, the workers will organize the Red Guard. . . . The leader of the revolution in all its stages

is the Communist Party. . . . Under the dictatorship all the Capitalist parties—Republican, Democratic, Progressive, [La Follette type] Socialist, etc.,—will be liquidated, the Communist Party alone functioning as the Party of the toiling masses. Likewise, will be dissolved all other organizations that are political props of all bourgeois rule, including chambers of commerce, employer's associations, rotary clubs, American Legion, Y.M.C.A., and such fraternal orders as the Masons, Odd Fellows, Elks, Knights of Columbus, etc. (p. 275).

This is the real meaning behind "Communism as the twentieth century version of Jeffersonian democracy."

Some words must be said about the implication in Justice Douglas' opinion that the law upheld by the majority decision hardly differs from the law of the Soviet state, as expressed by Vishinsky when he said: "In our state, naturally there can be no place for freedom of speech, press, and so on for the foes of socialism."

It would be difficult to find in the annals of the Supreme Court an observation so unjustifiable and injudicious. Hardly anything could be more explicit in Judge Medina's instructions to the jury, in Judge Hand's opinion, and in Justice Vinson's majority decision than the continually reiterated assertion: "It is perfectly lawful and proper for the defendants or anyone else to advocate reforms and changes in the laws, which seem to them to be salutary and necessary. No one has suggested that the defendants transgressed any laws by advocating such reforms and changes. No syllable of the indictment refers to any such matters."

The charge was not conspiracy to advocate the abolition of capitalism or the establishment of socialism. The charge bore on the advocacy of, and conspiracy to advocate the use of, force and violence to overthrow the state irrespective of the economic program of the defendants. Justice Douglas must surely be able to see the difference between denying a man certain freedoms to propose economic change and denying him the freedom to advocate that these reforms be carried out by force and violence.

To be sure, every state must evaluate the rights of the individual by its consequences upon society or upon the rights of other individuals. That is why, in the interest of social welfare or national security, which expresses the rights of other individuals, any particular right might be abridged. No right can be unconditionally affirmed independently of how it affects the community. This is true both in a democracy and in a totalitarian dictatorship. What then is the difference?

The differences are many and fundamental. In a democracy the social welfare or national security in whose name a right may be abridged is determined by the community or its responsible representatives—responsible, in the sense that they can be removed. Freely given consent of the majority enters in a way completely absent in a dictatorship. Secondly, the processes by which the decision is made are open, so that the opposition can be heard. Third, the decision is limited, renewable, and abolishable. The mandate is not made in perpetuity. Fourth, a democracy, as Professor A. E. Ewing has well pointed out, regards the freedoms of the individual as possessing an intrinsic worth, essential to the integrity of the individual personality, itself the object of supreme worth, and therefore moves slowly, and reluctantly towards the abridgment of individual rights. It waits for periods of genuine crisis, of genuine, clear and present danger to the security and safety

of the community. A totalitarian dictatorship has no regard for the intrinsic worth of human freedom and personality and moves immediately, brutally, and arbitrarily towards suppression of all opposition which threatens not the security of the community but the monopoly of physical power and intellectual authority of the dictatorship.

We have previously pointed out that *from the point of view of a democrat* one has a moral right to advocate the use of force and violence in a dictatorship where the processes do not exist which make possible the removal of evils and injustices. Again from the point of view of a democrat, one has no moral right to advocate the use of force and violence against the democratic community if, as a consequence of open and honest processes of inquiry, discussion, and decision, it is possible to remove evils and injustices.

In short we must reject Justice Douglas' comparison of Vishinsky's dictum with the law as expressed by his colleagues on the Supreme Court Bench as a gratuitous piece of demagogic rhetoric no less injudicious and irresponsible because it is made by a member of the highest judiciary body in the land.

The Smith Act is imperfectly phrased. Were it to be interpreted literally it could easily lend itself to abuse. The main, if not avowed, purposes of the Act —to prevent the organization of the Communist conspiracy from growing to a point where it could become dangerous, to make known to the people of the United States the nature of the Communist movement so that individuals who joined it would know what they were getting themselves into—could have been achieved by invoking other legislation, particularly the provision calling for the registration of agents of a foreign government. An overwhelming case could have been made out in court for the indictment of the Communist Party of the U.S.A. as an agency of the Soviet regime, and of every member who continued in it, as an agent of a foreign power. Although the listing of such agents would carry no *legal* sanctions, it is not likely that any but the hardened core of conspirators would be prepared to flaunt publicly the fact of their primary allegiance to an enemy power of their native country. The Communist Party would, of course, seek to mask itself behind other organizations, but it would do that less successfully than it does today. The Progressive Party and the American Labor Party in New York are today notorious Communist Party fronts but they cannot be molested under the Smith Act because they are careful to avoid teaching or advocating the desirability of revolutionary overthrow. Nor would they—(or should they)—be molested under the Foreign Agents Registration Act. But if the mechanism by which they were set up were ever publicly exposed, those individuals who moved behind the scenes might be required to be listed under the Foreign Agents Registration Act.

Nonetheless the Supreme Court has so interpreted the Smith Act as to really amend it. Advocacy of violent overthrow is illegal only when such advocacy constitutes a clear and present danger to the security of our democracy. The general principle behind that interpretation is unassailable except in the eyes of those ritualistic liberals who have forsaken the primary tenet in the faith of a liberal, *viz., the use of intelligence* to determine which of the conflicting claims behind the conflict of rights is to receive priority. A way should be found to leave the determination of the fact that a clear and present danger exists to the jury or to Congress, instead of making this subject to legal determination by the bench at any level.

Although the wisdom of enacting the Smith Law was doubtful, the wisdom of now repealing it is even more doubtful. For if the Smith Act were repealed it would give a new lease of life to an illusion whose widespread and pernicious character was to a not inconsiderable degree responsible for the original enactment of the law. This illusion is that the Communist Party is a political party like any other on the American scene, and therefore entitled to the same political rights and privileges as all other American political parties. It is amazing how pervasive this attitude has been among certain circles, especially in the colleges and universities. Here is a man who applies for a commission in the Army, a research post in a key plant, an important professorship in which he has an opportunity to influence thousands. If he has the technical qualifications, he is entitled to the position no matter whether he is a member of the Republican or Democratic or Socialist Party. Given knowledge of what these parties are, there can be no doubt about this. But, then, nine times out of ten one hears—or used to hear—"and since the Communist Party is a legal party, just like any other, a member of the Communist Party is also entitled to the post for which he has technical qualifications, just like anyone else."

That the Communist Party, although legal, was an organized conspiratorial movement to destroy the structure of freedom in every aspect of political and cultural life, was either not known or ignored. As a result of the court trials held under the Smith Act, the facts about the Communist Party have become widely known. These facts enjoy the authority of having proven themselves in the sharp debate and prolonged inquiry of the legal process. To repeal the Smith Act instead of continuing the process of reasonable amendment would probably lead many to assume, either that the Communist Party had changed its character, or that it did not really advocate the overthrow of democratic institutions by force and violence. Both assumptions would be false.

So long as the cold war rages between the Soviet Union and the democratic West, the Smith Act, now the law of the land, can by amendment and intelligent enforcement serve a therapeutic function without endangering the tradition of American rights and liberties.

In the long run, however, neither laws nor security agencies, as necessary as they are, can constitute a lasting defence of democratic institutions, if the will to freedom is not strong in a people. On several occasions the world has observed the consequences of the absence of a firm commitment to freedom on the part of governments and peoples. The Weimar Republic and Czechoslovakia are both illustrations of what happens when citizens idly watch conspirators paralyze the defensive powers of a democracy, avoid the fatiguing task of exposing and struggling against the conspirators in their multifarious guises and activities in the shop, on the street, in the schools, and rely mainly on the protective arm of the state itself infected with the germs of conspiracy.

Even when the democratic state itself is vigorous and free of infiltration, the legitimate desire to extirpate conspiracy, especially where it is allied with an external enemy, may lead it into adopting hasty administrative and legislative measures. These may have consequences prejudicial to the functioning of free institutions unless the rank and file citizens themselves preserve a democratic atmosphere in public and social life which encourages criticism and correction of governmental errors or excesses, and which at the same time limits the receptiveness to conspiracy. This requires participation of individuals and voluntary association on every level of political and social life. There is no short cut to, or guarantee of, intelligent participation—or enlightened public opinion. It is best furthered by an enlightened public education.

This is particularly true of the United States. The public schools on every level, including the private college, have played the most powerful role in the symbiotic process which has knit the United States into a unified culture. A unified culture, as distinct from a uniform one, recognizes that diversity of religion, cosmic outlook, local customs and personal belief are compatible with a common acceptance of the basic political patterns of democratic behavior.

Today our educational institutions have, if anything, an even more important role. If faith in freedom, and reliance on intelligence in settling problems, are to be strengthened during the long years of anxiety and danger ahead, it is to the schools we must look to develop the values, habits and attitudes which constitute the free man's second nature.

✓Zechariah Chafee, Jr.: FREEDOM AND FEAR

The foreword to Barth's Loyalty of Free Men *was written by the late Zechariah Chafee, Jr., an authority on free speech who was then near the end of his third-of-a-century tenure at Harvard Law School. During the hearings in Congress on the Mundt-Nixon Bill which became the McCarran Act, Chafee expressed strong disapproval of the proposed legislation, of the Smith Act, and of all tendencies to curtail free speech. Subsequent to the passage of the bill over President Truman's veto, Chafee became one of its foremost critics.*

ONE of the early sections [of the McCarran Act], 4 (a), has nothing to do with the registration of "Communist organizations." It threatens with ten years in prison anybody who commits a novel and vague political crime:

It shall be unlawful for any person knowingly to combine, conspire, or agree with any other person to perform any act which would contribute to the establishment within the United States of a totalitarian dictatorship, . . . the direction and control of which is to be vested in, or exercised by or under the dominion or control of, any foreign government, foreign organization, or foreign individual.

However, it is not an offense to propose a constitutional amendment.

Whatever this crime means, it goes far beyond the speech which has hitherto been punishable, even under the Smith Act. Nobody knows how unexpectedly a sedition law can be construed unless he has studied into such matters. The draftsman and the legislators have some specific situations in mind, but the actual use of the statute may be against some kind of conduct they never dreamed of. Thus a New York statute which was passed after the assassination of President McKinley to punish anarchists has never been used against an anarchist, but it was drastically enforced against Gitlow and other Communists, who are at the opposite pole of political thought from anarchists. So you cannot tell what sort of people will ever be punished for agreeing to aid in establishing a totalitarian dictatorship, but you can be sure that they will be very different people from anybody Congress had in mind in the summer of 1950.

We came through the perilous months between the fall of France and Pearl Harbor without needing any such peacetime sedition law to protect us against the mighty totalitarian dictatorship of Hitler, and we certainly do not need this fantastic law now.

The procedure of registration operates in two successive stages:

1. The Subversive Activities Control Board of five members receives a petition from the Attorney General against the organization alleged to be "Communist-action" or "Communist-front," holds public hearings with benefit of counsel, and either dismisses the case or orders the organization to register. Individuals may also be ordered by the Board to register if not listed by the "Communist-action organization" to which they are found to belong. In addition, a method is provided for an organization or a listed

officer or member to get off the register.

2. Either side can get judicial review in the Court of Appeals in the District of Columbia, and after that in the Supreme Court if it is willing to bother with the case. After the courts have upheld the Board (or no appeal has been filed) the order to register becomes final. Then the disagreeable consequences of registration go into effect.

It is my well-considered opinion that the Board is going to do the real deciding in most cases against "Communist-front organizations." Except for passing on constitutional issues, judicial review is not likely to be of much value to a group which has lost its case in the Board. In the first place, going to court is expensive. The financial resources of these propagandist enterprises, schools for adult radicals, etc., are often small anyway; and they will be further crippled by the denial of income tax advantages under the Act, which is likely to scare off contributors as soon as proceedings start, without waiting for the final order. Second, all the evidence against the attacked group or on its behalf will be taken before the Board. No judge will hear any witnesses. Now, any lawyer knows that the way in which testimony shapes up depends considerably upon the competence, experience, and fairness of the person or persons conducting the actual trial. Third, even if a condemned group can afford to appeal, the courts will not have much of a chance to reverse the Board's decision, unless on some constitutional ground. The definition of a "Communist-front organization" in the Act is so wide and vague that it will be hard for judges to say that the Board was wrong in bringing the group within that definition. Busy judges will probably be reluctant to substitute their own judgment for the judgment of the officials who heard the testimony which fills thousands of pages.

Therefore, the way the McCarran Act will operate depends very largely on the five persons composing the Subversive Activities Control Board. What are they going to be like down the years? They are appointed by the President for staggered terms of three years, confirmed by the Senate, and eligible for reappointment. Not more than three can belong to the same political party. Despite the short term, some measure of independence is assured by the provision that they cannot be removed for any reason except neglect of duty or malfeasance in office. The salary is $15,000 a year, and they are not to "engage in any other business, vocation, or employment."

I do not mean to question in any way the character and competence of the present members of the Subversive Activities Control Board. Harry P. Cain deserves especial credit for warning the country in a public address that "in an effort to keep our Nation secure at home, we have constructed an apparatus which can destroy us if we don't watch out." Yet we have to remember that a new broom sweeps clean. The personnel of the Federal Trade Commission and many other federal or state administrative bodies has tended to run downhill, after the first few years when able men were attracted by the opportunity to get new work started. The future composition of the Subversive Activities Control Board will present the same risk.

Enormous powers over the lives of private citizens are possessed by the five men on this Board. They can shape political action, blast reputations, make government employees and workmen lose their jobs with small hope of getting other employment.

Only a terrible danger to the nation

could justify Congress in placing these enormous powers in the hands of five men who do not have the training and experience of judges or the life-tenure which the Constitution considers essential to assure the independence of men who make vital decisions. Does such a terrible danger really exist?

Perhaps something can be said for requiring all political parties to register, and all organizations which are somehow associated with politics; but the McCarran Act singles out particular political groups to bear heavy burdens from which the rest are wholly free. Imagine what it would mean if the Republican Party alone or the Democratic Party alone had to file the names and addresses of all its members with the Department of Justice, and repeat this full list every year, while for every omitted name or address the party officers would go to prison.

But those are good parties, say the supporters of this Act; it hits only bad parties. By the American tradition, sifting bad parties from good parties is the job of the voters, and not the job of Congress or government officials. We have hitherto had confidence that most of the voters would recognize a bad party when they saw it and keep away from it. The fate of the Know-Nothing Party, which incited prejudice against recent immigrants, and the failure of the Communist Party to win an election to any federal, state or city office for years and years, show that this confidence in the voters is amply justified.

Nevertheless, in 1950 and 1954, while France and Italy were managing to recover from devastating defeats in spite of scores of Communists in their national legislatures, the Congress of the victorious United States rushed through two long and complicated laws in order to outlaw a political party which is so nearly dead that it has not nominated a

candidate of its own for President since 1940. As Senator Carter Glass remarked, "What's the use of wasting dynamite when insect-powder will do?"

It is argued that, although the Communist Party amounts to nothing in elections, it still exists as an organization making policies and spreading propaganda of a bad sort, and hence it is necessary to break it up completely. No doubt, this purpose will be accomplished if the Supreme Court affirms the Board's registration order. There will no longer be any organization called the Communist Party of America. Yet how much good will that really do? The present actual Communists will be no less harmful than they are now. They will continue to have the same ideas. The prime cause of all dangerous political agitation is discontent, and outlawing men does nothing to remove their discontent. Quite the contrary.

There is no reason to expect that the order of five government officials is going to stop Americans who are Communists at heart from meeting together in some way or other. Anybody who has studied the history of Irish societies in the days of Daniel O'Connell can tell pretty well what will happen. Every time a particular society was declared unlawful, it was promptly dissolved and its former members started a new society for exactly the same purposes. The Communist Party may reorganize under a different name, as Mr. Truman predicted, or perhaps it will split into a number of Shakespearean Societies, Dante Institutes, chess clubs, indoor baseball associations, etc. Whatever occurs, the Subversive Activities Control Board will have to engage in a series of wild-goose chases. And, meanwhile, we shall no longer know whether there are 70,000 Communists or 700,000.

Moreover, this law merely scratches the surface of the biggest danger from the presence of Communists inside a free country. That danger comes, not from the mass of Party members, but from embittered and fanatical individuals who, regardless of carrying cards in any organization, are eager to engage in wicked and desperate acts which will aid the Soviet Union. The Report of the Canadian Royal Commission on atomic spies shows how much harm a few men can do. The more recent Report of the Australian Royal Commission in 1955, which investigated the documents from Moscow turned over by Petrov after he left the Soviet Embassy in Canberra, also tells much about the Communist spy system. This report shows how spies operated under the direction of M.V.D. officials in the Embassy, who were specifically charged with espionage, and that the system had very slight connections with the Communist Party of Australia:

Quite apart from the known Party members, the auxiliary force [of Australians] comprises some persons whose role it is to conceal their Communist affiliations and sympathies and to operate in the guise of ordinary loyal Australian citizens. This class provides the most dangerous pool of helpers in fifth-column and espionage work, and it is amongst this class that the Moscow Centre [the headquarters for the conduct of espionage work abroad] usually looks for aid.

[From] the material before us we think it unlikely the Australian Communist Party, as a Party, had any connection with Soviet espionage here.

Generally speaking, the M.V.D. [the Ministry of Internal Affairs in charge of non-military espionage outside the Soviet Union] is disinclined to use the known and prominent Communist Party member as a direct agent. His use is chiefly as a "talent spotter." The prominent Party member is likely to be known to counter-intelligence organizations, and the risk of compromising the Communist Party is one not lightly to be taken. It is the secret or "under cover" Party member or the sympathizer, who is not a member of the Party who is preferred, because his activities are less likely to be subject to the scrutiny of counter-intelligence. There is evidence that latterly the rule against using the known Communist has become more strict.

Aren't we barking up the wrong tree when we worry so much about publicly known Communist organizations and their meetings? The entire government testimony against the eleven top-string leaders at the 1950 trial before Judge Medina in New York City, as reported in the New York *Times*, contains a lot of silly talk at meetings, of a very exasperating sort, but nothing was said or done which would make any sane citizen lie awake at night a single minute. Spies and saboteurs do not make speeches at such affairs. If they meet at all, it is only in very small groups by secret arrangement. The registration or outlawing or dissolution of an organization of thousands of talkative comrades is not going to remove the evil from the minds of men who are ready to brave prison and death out of hatred toward their own government.

The "Communist-action" provisions of the McCarran Act are a bad precedent for future legislation. No major party is likely to try to wipe out the other major party, as the Federalists did in 1798; but both major parties may be tempted to join forces in order to cripple or kill a third party with enough strength to be annoying, especially in state or city elections. For the first time in our history, we have written into law an ingenious device to accomplish this object. The people in power in the two major parties frame a definition of a bad political party. They do this by picking characteristics of an objectionable sort which are possessed by some members of the party they want to smash. Then they brand the whole party with those objectionable characteristics, and consequently make it carry a heavy load in the political race against competing parties which run unburdened.

Now, this may seem very clever when it is used against parties with a Communistic tinge, but it is a game anybody can play at. Once this law gets people accustomed to the method of having officials sift out "bad" parties instead of letting the voters do it themselves, other laws can be drafted with new definitions of badness to hit some party which has nothing to do with communism. There is no logical limit to the possibility of this proscribing an opposition party, for every party has some members with qualities capable of arousing intense and widespread detestation. Even the Republican Party in its early years included many prominent Abolitionists who had vigorously advocated violations of the Fugitive Slave Law, and some of them had overthrown the operation of the law by force and violence in the streets of Boston. The Democrats and the Southern Whigs would have found the device in the McCarran Act very useful for strangling the Republican Party in its cradle. And it can easily be used in the future to get rid of some new third party to which many honest and patriotic citizens belong. In order "to preserve our free institutions" and the processes of self-government, Congress and the American people ought to repudiate the vicious device once and for all.

Inasmuch as this part of the McCarran Act is likely to reach many groups whose purposes are cultural as well as political and who are engaged in exchanging ideas rather than winning elections, the interference with the lives of private citizens is much more extensive than in the case of the "Communist-action" provisions.

Here again, there is something to be said for a general registration law requiring all groups which attempt to influence public opinion to disclose the pertinent facts about themselves through systematic procedures. The harmfulness of non-disclosure is by no means confined to "Communist-front organizations." For instance, virulent anti-Semitic circulars and pamphlets falsely and libelously accusing long lists of well-known, decent citizens of disloyalty are often widely mailed by organizations with high-sounding names, which frequently take good care not to mention their authors and the men who put up the money. A broad statute to break through this vicious anonymity of defamers of every sort is recommended in the 1947 Report of the President's Committee on Civil Rights. On the other hand, I seriously question whether such a statute will be a desirable remedy for this evil; it is likely to be enforced inefficiently and in a haphazard way, and to stifle more good views than bad views. At all events, if Congress thinks a compulsory disclosure law for propaganda is needed, than it is needed for all sides of political, racial, and religious controversies. Such a law should seek to force into broad daylight all the enemies of democracy and not just a particular portion of them as in the McCarran Act, leaving the rest to remain in the darkness they love, "because their ways are evil."

Leaving the lopsidedness of this part of the Act for later attention, let us see what effect registration of a group as "Communist-front" will have upon its capacity to do effective work. Take a labor school as an illustration. Every teacher, every student, every contributor to its support has good reason to expect that the law will treat him as a "member" of the organization. Hence, as already stated, any person who is asked to teach or study at this labor school or to give it some money knows that, if he does so, he will encounter difficulties in getting or holding a job with the government or in a defense plant. He cannot go abroad for lack of a passport. His contributions to the school will not be deductible for income tax purposes. When pamphlets or form letters come to him from the school, the envelopes will be labeled *"Communist Organization,"* which will make a very bad impression on any business associates or fellow-tenants in his apartment-house who happen to glance at his mail. This novel stigma on enterprises which have violated no law recalls the practice of medieval princes to require Jews to wear special marks or colors on their coats.

So after the labor school registers, very few people will be willing to teach or study there or give it one cent.

Even those who gave money to a social or propagandist enterprise *before* registration or who no longer participate in its work may still be classed by the law as "members." This is often done by Congressional investigating committees, and there is no formal procedure, either in ordinary life or in the McCarran Act, for terminating one's loose relationship with such enterprises. This uncertainty as to how you get out, once you become a member, is likely to make prudent people refuse to have anything at all to do with enterprises which might conceivably be ordered to register. And as soon as the Board starts a proceeding to compel an organization to register, many former contributors, if they are prudent, will try to announce as publicly as possible that they will have no further dealings with the organization.

All this virtually outlaws whatever groups are asked to register. Even if an enterprise is able to survive, it will have lost most of its moderate members and be wholly in the hands of extremists who don't care. Its unobjectionable activities will be crippled. Whatever it still does will be more radical than ever.

First, I should like to point out the great dangers of thus interfering by law with freedom of discussion through organizations. The Act proposes to twist out of all recognizable shape one of the leading traditions of American life: the possibility of freely forming associations for all sorts of purposes—religious, political, social, and economic.

If we look back over our national history, we see that many of the most significant political and social changes began with the efforts of some small informal group disliked by the ordinary run of citizens. The abolition of slavery grew out of Garrison's Antislavery Society and similar associations. The Nineteenth Amendment is the culmination of the activities of a few unpopular women in the middle of the last century. The popular election of Senators, the federal income tax, and several other reforms largely originated with the Grangers and the Populists. American political, social, and economic institutions have developed to a very large extent through the interaction of propagandist groups. The appearance of a group favoring one side of an issue often aroused a group of opponents, and the public profited from its opportunity to judge between the competing presentations of both sides of an important national problem. Under modern conditions, freedom of speech under the First Amendment is likely to be ineffective if it means only the liberty of an isolated individual to talk about his ideas. Indeed, from the very beginning, freedom of speech has involved the liberty of a number of individuals to associate themselves for the advocacy of a common purpose whether they exchange ideas in a hall or by mail like the Committees of Correspondence before the Revolution. Thus, freedom of speech and freedom of assembly fit into each other. They are both related to the possibility of petitioning Congress and the state legislators for redress of grievances, which is only part of the wider freedom to submit the views of the individual or the group to the people at large for judgment.

It may be argued, however, that the so-called "Communist-front organizations" present an entirely new problem because they have objectionable purposes and include objectionable persons in their membership. This brings me to my second point. It has always been true of a great many propagandist organizations that their purposes were denounced by numerous law-abiding citizens and that their memberships included some extremists whose actions or ideas were open to serious adverse criticism. The books are full of denunciations by prominent citizens of abolitionists, women suffragists, labor unions, Populists, etc., which would more than match anything which has been written about the Joint Anti-Fascist Refugee Committee or the National Lawyers Guild or any of the other contemporary organizations classed as "subversive" by the House Un-American Activities Committee and the Attorney General's list.

The membership situation is much the same now as it has always been. Propagandist organizations are not likely to be made up of men and women with conventional ideas. The very nature of a propagandist organization is that it wants to change something; obviously, then, it is likely to be made up of the kind of people who do want change.

Such people vary a good deal. The core of the propagandist organization often consists of those whom Woodrow Wilson described as "forward-looking men and women," who disagree with the complacency of the ordinary run of citizens about some issue but still are fairly moderate in the changes they desire and so do not seriously offend their neighbors. Yet these are rarely the only members of a propagandist organization; it is likely also to include what Theodore Roosevelt called "the lunatic fringe." The organizations opposed to slavery had members who urged violations of law, such as rescuing fugitive slaves and transporting them to Canada on the Underground Railway. Some of them even favored or participated in the attempt of John Brown to start a slave-rising in Virginia. Time and again the whole labor movement has been denounced as lawless because some unionists undoubtedly engaged in violence against their employers and non-union workers. Saloons were smashed by some prohibitionists, like Carry Nation. It is plain that there is nothing new in the adherence of extremists to organizations with desirable or at least legitimate purposes.

Hence, we should not be surprised or frightened if some contemporary organizations for upholding the rights of minorities get some members who are more in sympathy with communism than the rank and file of the organization like. It is equally possible that organizations for upholding free speech or a fair trial or other fundamental constitutional rights may attract extremists whose interest is not in constitutional rights but in getting a Communist off. In short, it is inevitable that the membership of organizations formed to bring about change should include some persons who want a great deal of change.

The supporters of this law assume that the moderate members of an organization always have an obligation to oust the extremists or else resign themselves. But this is by no means plain. Throughout the history of this country, the propagandist organizations which I have been describing were engaged in a hard fight against determined opponents. Their chances of winning this fight would clearly have been weakened if they had also waged an internal war with their own extremists or if moderates had got out and stopped supporting the cherished purpose of the organization. The practical question must have arisen hundreds of times: Was it better to put up with the extremists and continue the fight for an important cause, or disrupt the organization and probably kill the cause?

Now, what would have happened in the history of our country if the policy of the McCarran Act had been embodied in law during the Nineteenth Century? There would have been different tests, of course, aimed at the kind of organization whose purpose was hated by the authorities of the particular period. Yet the general principle would have been exactly the same. The idea is to condemn an organization because of the objectionable ideas or conduct of its extremists and thus make it difficult for the moderates in the organization to accomplish their basic purpose. For example, suppose that the standards of permissible membership in anti-slavery societies had been fixed by a board chosen by slaveowners and the owners of Northern cotton mills. Again, suppose that the associations of employers and their friends in Congress had been able to set up a board to outlaw a trade union affiliated with men devoted to industrial violence.

When the membership and policies of an opinion-forming organization can be judged and controlled by outsiders with governmental power, all sorts of opportunities for the suppression of legitimate ideas arise. The officials, being outsiders, may be rather unsympathetic with the legitimate purposes of the organization. There is a tremendous temptation to opponents of those legitimate purposes to influence the selection and the behavior of the controlling officials. The presence of extremists can easily be made an excuse for outlawing an organization when *the real reason for getting rid of it is not fear of the extremists but hatred of the legitimate purposes.* The organization is suppressed, not because it might promote a revolution but because it might win elections and produce legislation.

There are many important questions to be settled in this country today, with much to be said on both sides. Take four illustrations: (1) Should we (a) favor the transfer to a different government (or perhaps the abolition) of one of the permanent seats on the United Nations Security Council, or (b) support its occupancy by the government of Chiang Kai-shek as one of the five Great Powers? (2) Should we (a) stop economic aid to Franco in Spain unless he establishes free and unfettered elections and liberty of the press and religion, or (b) keep on paying millions of dollars to help a totalitarian regime? (3) Should we (a) force states which still want racial segregation in schools and places of entertainment to get rid of it very soon, or (b) allow them to end it very gradually when local public opinion is willing to accept a change? (4) Should we (a) repeal the McCarran Act, or (b) enforce it vigorously and bring about a great many registrations of groups as "Communist-front organizations"? These are vital questions, on which honest and reasonable men differ. They cannot be wisely decided unless individuals and opinion-forming organizations on one side are as free to present their views as are those on the other side.

The significant thing is that in every one of these questions an organization which takes the (b) side cannot possibly be touched by the Act, while any organization which takes the (a) side can conceivably be outlawed. Although there are plenty of honest reasons why many patriotic American citizens stand for the (a) side, it happens in every case that this side coincides with the views of the Soviet Union and its supporters, whose reasons are quite different. One of the factors which the Subversive Activities Control Board can take into consideration in determining whether an organization is "Communist-front" is:

(4) the extent to which the positions taken or advanced by it from time to time on matters of policy do not deviate from those of any Communist political organization, Communist foreign government, or the world Communist movement . . .

Thus, this Act leaves organizations on the (b) side untouched, no matter if they include Fascists, anti-Semites, and advocates of religious and racial hatred, and also greatly aids them by silencing a large number of their most vigorous opponents. Insofar as there are errors on the (b) side, the law will be increasing public danger enormously by making it very difficult for those errors to be combatted by reason.

Mr. Truman said that, because of the clause just quoted, the McCarran Act "can be the greatest danger to freedom of speech, press, and assembly, since the Alien and Sedition Laws of 1798."

This provision could easily be used to classify as a Communist-front organization any organization which is advocating a single policy or objective which is also being urged by the Communist Party or by a Communist foreign government. . . . Thus, an organization which advocates low-cost housing for sincere humanitarian reasons might be classified as a Communist-front organization because the Communists regularly exploit slum conditions as one of their fifth-column techniques.

Actual experience amply justifies the expectation that the vague characterization of "Communist-front organizations" in this law will be used to cripple or suppress many organizations which serve very desirable purposes, even if they do include some leftist people among their supporters. The ease with which a very useful organization can be condemned under a similar loose definition on the basis of very thin evidence is shown by Professor Walter Gellhorn of Columbia in an article relating to the wholly unfounded red-listing of the Southern Conference for Human Welfare by the House Un-American Activities Committee.

Remember always that everything depends on the five men who make up the Subversive Activities Control Board as the years go by. Equally important is the attitude of the Attorney General for the time being. Just by filing a petition against any enterprise he dislikes, he can put it under a black cloud which will scare off contributors and force it to interrupt its normal activities in order to defend itself for months before the Board at the cost of thousands of dollars. This is enough to wreck almost any group even though it eventually escapes registration.

Thus the McCarran Act has a lopsided effect on the formation of public opinion. It creates a tremendous risk of outlawing a considerable number of groups of law-abiding people with inquiring minds, engaged in furthering some end which they believe to be in the very best interests of the United States. And, on the other hand, this law will encourage those who hate the purposes of such groups to do all they can to suppress or hamper them by influencing the selection of new members of the Subversive Activities Control Board and by bringing pressure of every sort upon the officials on the Board. The "Communist-front" provisions violate the fundamental principle of self-government that the persons in power for the time being ought not to be able to shape public opinion in their favor by force.

Very likely propagandist groups do exist among us for the support of measures which would hurt the nation if they were adopted. Yet that has always been true in our history. If we wipe out the law requiring "Communist-front organiza-tions" to register, we can rely, as in the past, on the good sense of the American people to choose among competing policies after getting the benefit of full discussion unhampered by government officials.

The only way to preserve "the existence of free American institutions" is to make free institutions a living force. To ignore them in the very process of purporting to defend them, as frightened men urge, will leave us little worth defending.

We must choose between freedom and fear—we cannot have both. If the citizens of the United States persist in being afraid, the real rulers of this country will be fanatics fired with a zeal to save grown men from objectionable ideas by putting them under the care of official nurse-maids.

Walter Gellhorn: FREE SPEECH AND THE COMMUNIST CONSPIRACY

Recognized as one of the foremost authorities on administrative law and on civil liberties, Walter Gellhorn has also been active in the American Civil Liberties Union, the NAACP, and in agencies of the federal government. After serving as law secretary to Justice Harlan F. Stone (1931-32), he joined the faculty of Columbia Law School, where he now teaches. Reprinted here is his effort rationally and comprehensively to evaluate the "Communist Menace" and the legislation passed to deal with it.

THE American system of government rests on a theory that, to some people, has always seemed the height of foolishness. The nation has bet its life upon the proposition that "right conclusions are more likely to be gathered out of a multitude of tongues, than through any kind of authoritative selection."

The American Constitution in unconditional language says that the freedom of speech and of the press should not be abridged. The soundness of the principle underlying that brave declaration is now once more undergoing an agonizing reappraisal. The world, contorted by a clash of ideologies, lives in fear that the war

Reprinted with permission of The Macmillan Company from *American Rights: The Constitution* by Walter Gellhorn (New York, 1960), pp. 70-71, 74-75, 82-84, 88-95. Copyright 1960 by Walter Gellhorn.

of words and ideas may become in fact a ruinous war between nations. The tensions aroused by that fear stir impatience with the traditional counsels of toleration. Free trade in ideas, many people feel, is a supportable policy when the times are quiet and when there is ample opportunity for a ruminative exchange of views. But when desperate perils may be near at hand, a diversity of ideas comes to be regarded as divisive, and dissent comes to be equated with disaffection. Then arises a demand for modification of the faith reflected in constitutional provisions like those now under discussion.

This demand at present draws not only its inspiration but its chief justification from the ambiguous character of the Communist Party. The "class war" is more than a figure of speech to Communists. They deem themselves to be engaged here and now in a war against the existing social order, for which they wish to substitute their own dictatorship. To that end they—or, at least, some of them—are able to justify in their own minds the use of tactics that bear no relationship to the ordinary contests for power within a democratic framework. Identifying their cause with that of the Soviet Union, they have faithfully followed the convolutions of policies designed by that great power for its own national interests alone. Politically-inspired espionage on behalf of the Soviet Union has been proved beyond doubt in a number of dramatic instances. Infiltration of labor unions and other organizations has occurred so that they might be maneuvered not for the interests of their members or in furtherance of their declared purposes, but in order to advance a cause to which the membership has not knowingly given its allegiance. Guile and stealth have been used to intensify rather than to lessen the frictions that inevitably arise in a complex society, so that dissension may be aroused and faith in governmental processes may be diminished.

But along with the clandestine, conspiratorial, criminal, and corrupt activities which the Communists justify as unpleasant necessities in the class struggle, can be found another aspect of the Communist Party. It seeks to function as an open and public organization, devoted to political agitation unrelated to violence. It propagandizes as do other political parties. It appeals for votes. It attempts to gain adherents by persuasion. It appeals to the discontented and the disillusioned, promising (as do other political parties) that its program will end their difficulties.

Many supporters of democratic principles are unable to distinguish between the two aspects of the Communist Party. Political activity by Communist zealots, they maintain, is a deceptive device. The Communists, these persons say, do not really intend to debate ideas and to abide by majority conclusions; their advocacy is intended not to enlighten judgment but to create internal disaffection; their aim is not persuasion of the present majority, but the development of an atmosphere in which a militant minority can seize power; hence, even their seemingly innocent words and deeds must be regarded as steps in a totalitarian conspiracy aimed at destroying the freedom the Constitution is dedicated to preserving. It matters not that their number is small—according to official estimates that some observers believe to be four times too high, only 25,000 in the United States, a nation of over 170,000,000. These few, it is argued, are so singleminded, so totally committed to their cause that they constitute a grave and continuing threat to constitutional liberties. . . .

Before turning to the issues that touch

directly upon freedom of expression, we may usefully note that undesirable conduct—as distinct from words—is already interdicted by many laws. Thus, for example, penal statutes deal firmly with crimes of action (such as sabotage) and with crimes of stealth (such as espionage and disclosure of official information). Violence, whether or not aimed at overthrow of the government, is not tolerated. The ingress of aliens who might endanger the nation is regulated, and contact is maintained with the aliens who have been allowed to enter. The domestic agents of any "foreign principal" are required to register with the Department of Justice, and to disclose their activities in behalf of their principal. . . .

But measures like these have not completely quieted concern. In America, perhaps more acutely than in most other countries, the feeling has been manifested that since Communist beliefs may give rise to dangers that might not be detected until too late, the nation's defense requires suppressing the teaching and advocacy of Communism itself. If Soviet espionage agents are likely to be recruited from those who are now or who in future might become Communists, then those who are pro-Communist must be exposed and recruitment of converts must be blocked. Views like these underlie the measures that seek to restrict belief and utterance, and that attempt to stigmatize individuals not for their positive deeds but for their supposed allegiances. . . .

THE SMITH ACT: ILLEGAL ADVOCACY

. . . Not until 1948 was this law turned against the Communists, who were undoubtedly its chief targets when it was adopted. In 1941 it had first been used as the basis of prosecuting a small group of Marxists who were strongly anti-Stalin and anti-Soviet; believers in civil liberties protested its use on that occasion, though the Communists were apparently untroubled so long as their enemies were being harassed. In 1943 the law was used in a sedition trial against twenty-eight alleged Nazi sympathizers; again civil libertarians protested, while the Communists were silent. Neither of these cases reached the Supreme Court. In 1948, however, an indictment based upon the statute was lodged against eleven top leaders of the Communist Party in the United States. After a long and dramatic trial had resulted in their conviction, they appealed to the higher courts. Ultimately, in *Dennis* v. *United States,* the Supreme Court upheld the constitutionality of the law and sustained the convictions. . . .

The aftermath of the *Yates* case is interesting. By the end of 1956 convictions of Communist leaders under the Smith Act had numbered 114. Many of these cases were still pending in the appellate courts when the *Yates* decision was announced in June of 1957. On one ground or another, convictions were set aside and new trials were granted to many of these defendants. The Department of Justice itself dropped the prosecution of a considerable number, on the ground that they could not properly be convicted on the basis of the evidence now available. Most significantly of all, the cases against the nine remaining defendants in *Yates,* as to whom the Supreme Court had refused to dismiss the charges, were abandoned by the prosecution because there was insufficient evidence that they had advocated action as distinct from opinion. After all the clamor, after all the expressed alarm about the peril into which the United States was being plunged by this handful of misguided fanatics, the prosecution felt itself unable to show persuasively that the Communist spokesmen had engaged in the forbidden incitements to illegality.

This should stimulate a sober second look at the surface attractions of programs of suppression and coercion. Occasionally the supporters of these programs are scoundrels who falsely parade themselves as upholders of democracy; but more often they are good and sincere men. Men genuinely devoted to worthy ends sometimes endorse efforts to force unanimity of sentiment, not because they consciously espouse authoritarianism, but because they hope thus to assure maximum support for the nation and its people. No matter how well intentioned they may be, however, those efforts themselves create a graver danger than they overcome. The perils sought to be suppressed are regularly overestimated. History shows in one example after another how excessive have been the fears of earlier generations, who shuddered at menaces that, with the benefit of hindsight, we now know were mere shadows. This in itself should induce the modern generation to view with prudent skepticism the recurrent alarms about the fatal potentialities of dissent. In any event, in a world torn between the merits of freedom and the blandishments of totalitarian power, the lovers of freedom cannot afford to sacrifice their moral superiority by adopting totalitarian methods in order to create a self-deluding sense of security. Suppression, once accepted as a way of life, is likely to spread. It reinforces the herd urge toward orthodoxies of all kinds—religious, economic, and moral as well as political.

The sounder course . . . is to disregard advocacy and teaching, even though its ultimate goal may be acts, unless there is imminent danger that unlawful conduct will be induced. At a particular time and in particular circumstances a speaker may properly be deemed an actionist. Realistically considered, there can in fact be such an offense as inciting a riot; there can in fact be such an offense as organizing violent steps that are calculated to disturb public order or to lead to overthrow. The use of one's vocal cords or of one's typewriter may, therefore, properly be regarded as punishable action in some situations. Those situations, however, do not arise when there is still ample opportunity for the force of words to be dissipated by other and better words, or by feasible defensive measures, or (most significantly) by the course of events that the speaker does not control. The man who urges an angry mob to follow him into action, then and there, is creating an immediate threat to public safety. But a man who urges an audience to follow him into action when the time is ripe, at some uncertain date in the future, is not a present menace, though he may be a profound irritation. Two things argue against dealing with him or his kind at that stage. First, society should conserve its energies, using them only for real rather than supposititious problems. Second, when immediacy of danger is not the test, the boundaries between permissible and impermissible talk become too hard to draw. When that happens, the people at large are discouraged from talking at all about things that matter deeply, lest they be adjudged to have overstepped the lines. A free society can better stand the risks of talk than the risks of silence.

THE INTERNAL SECURITY ACT OF 1950: McCARRAN ACT

. . . The ultimate effects of the McCarran Act are difficult to gauge. Of course its sponsors meant that it should cripple the Communist movement in America. Perhaps it will have that result, though no one can yet say whether it will ever do more than lead to changes in name and appearance. President Truman, acting on the advice of the Departments of State, Defense, and Justice (of which the F.B.I. is a part), as well as the Central Intelligence Agency, sought unsuccessfully to prevent passage of the act; the government agencies asserted that their operations would be seriously damaged if, as they feared might happen, the Communists were to be "driven underground" and were forced to become an even more secret movement. Moreover, the act contains provisions of extremely doubtful practical wisdom—such as one directing the Secretary of Defense to publish a list of industrial establishments engaged in important military production, and forbidding any Communist to seek work in those establishments. The publication of such a list would very probably be warmly welcomed by hostile espionage agents, who would thus be spared the trouble of locating the nation's industrial nerve centers. But it is not the purpose here to debate the political consequences of the statute. We are now concerned solely with its bearing on political liberty.

Laws of this type must inevitably restrict the freedoms of speech and assembly. The McCarran Act, for example, sets forth, as one of the important criteria for judging the character of an organization brought before the Subversive Activities Control Board, the extent of its adherence to the expressed policies of the Soviet Union. Thus, if an organization were to devote itself to, say supporting the admission of Red China into the United Nations, or to control of nuclear weapons according to the Russian instead of the American prescription, or agitating for the withdrawal of American air bases from the periphery of the Soviet Union, it might at least conceivably have to face demands that it register as a Communist organization—for all of these are among the declared objectives of the Soviet Union, though all of them are also conscientiously supported by persons who have independently arrived at the same conclusions. If people cannot meet when they wish and espouse whatever views they choose, without risking the pains and penalties of forced registration, they are to that extent less free than they were before.

THE COMMUNIST CONTROL ACT
OF 1954

In 1954, the Congress of the United States grew impatient. The McCarran Act of 1950 had failed to bring about the demise of the supposed Communist Menace. The registration procedures required by that statute had proved to be just as cumbersome as President Truman had predicted they would be, when he had unsuccessfully tried to block enactment. So now a new effort was made, motivated partly by genuine exasperation and partly, it is believed, by the desire of certain "liberal" legislators to demonstrate that they were at least as vigorously anti-Communist as were their political opponents.

The Communist Control Act of 1954 has the announced purpose of "outlawing" the Communist Party in the United States; but thus far its consequences remain highly doubtful. The act begins by stating the Congressional conclusion that the Communist Party is not in fact a political organization, but is instead a conspiratorial and revolutionary movement that serves as agent of a hostile foreign government. As such, the Communist Party is declared to be a present and continuing danger to national security. This legislative finding, the statue continues, justifies withholding from that party any of the rights or privileges enjoyed by "legal bodies created under the laws." The statutory language is vague, but its sponsors declared at the time that it was intended, among other things, to prevent the Communist Party from making leases or contracts, from suing in the courts, or from appearing on the ballot.

Article I of the American Constitution provides, in Section 9, that "No Bill of Attainder or ex post facto Law shall be passed." An "ex post facto Law" is one which declares to be a crime conduct which was not illegal when it occurred. A bill of attainder, according to an important decision of the Supreme Court, is a legislative act, no matter what its form, that applies "either to named individuals or to easily ascertainable members of a group in such a way as to inflict punishment on them without a judicial trial." Measured by this test, the Communist Control Act of 1954 may readily be deemed unconstitutional as an attempt to punish an allegedly conspiratorial group without affording the group the protections of a trial. At least debatably, however, no "punishment" is involved in withdrawing recognition of an organization's legal status. Hence it may be well to consider the merits of the approach here taken by Congress, without predispositions based on constitutional provisions of uncertain applicability.

The chief issue, in my opinion, is the desirability of seeking to bar Communists (or any other unpopular group) from participating in the democratic process of elections. as of 1951, eight of

the states had excluded from a place on the ballot for state and local elections any party which used "Communist" in its name, or which was connected with the Communist Party of the United States; other states withheld electoral rights from groups that advocated forcible overthrow of the government. The validity of these laws was doubtful, and they did not appear to have any great impact upon political events. The 1954 federal statute now sought to do on a nation-wide basis what some of the states had been attempting in a piecemeal manner.

There is a superficial plausibility about denying to the enemies of democracy the opportunity to use its machinery. But, when the matter is considered more closely, the unreasonableness of this step becomes plain. The foundation stone upon which democratic institutions are built is the voters' opportunity to choose freely among competing candidates and programs. They may choose well or poorly, but they must be able to choose freely if democracy is to preserve its meaning. Moreover, if vote-seekers are flatly forbidden to make electoral appeals to vote-givers, strong support is lent to the argument that basic changes can never be achieved by democratic means, but must be produced by revolution.

Charles Evans Hughes made this point tellingly as long ago as 1920. A former Governor of New York, former Justice of the Supreme Court, and former Republican candidate for the presidency of the United States, Hughes—who subsequently became Secretary of State and, later, Chief Justice of the United States —did not hesitate to oppose the action of the New York legislature in refusing to allow five elected Socialists to take their seats, because in those days the Socialist

Party was deemed "subversive." When the ousted men appealed to the courts, Hughes appeared as counsel in behalf of the most prominent association of lawyers in New York, to support the Socialists' rights. He deemed it "a most serious mistake to proceed, not against individuals charged with violation of law, but against masses of our citizens combined for political action, by denying them the only recourse of peaceful government; that is, action by the ballot box and through duly elected representatives in legislative bodies." The question to be weighed, as this distinguished jurist so well saw, is not whether the aims of a political group are deeply obnoxious to the present majority; the question, rather, is whether the channels of peaceful persuasion shall be kept open so that there can never be justification for resort to force.

Another debatable provision of the 1954 statute adds "Communist-infiltrated organizations" to the categories of "Communist-action" and "Communist-front" groups that had been recognized by the McCarran Act of 1950. Like the other two types, "Communist-infiltrated" organizations are subjected to various burdens, requirements, and penalties. While general in form, this part of the new statute seems particularly directed at labor organizations, which, if found to be "Communist-infiltrated," are to lose the protections of the laws that compel employers to bargain collectively with their employees' chosen representatives. That is to say, even if workers freely chose to be represented by a condemned union, the employer could refuse to deal with it.

The term "Communist-infiltrated," added to the other adjectives that have been used to characterize groups in which Communists are thought to play a part, is obviously difficult to define. The statute says that it connotes an organization which has been substantially directed or controlled by individuals who within the past three years have been knowing Communists or foreign agents, and which has served within that period as a means of aiding or supporting the Communists or a foreign Communist government, or impairing America's military strength or industrial capacity. The Attorney General may file charges against such an organization, which is then entitled to a hearing before the Subversive Activities Control Board created by the McCarran Act of 1950.

The first proceeding initiated by the Attorney General under this branch of the statute illustrates both the possible uses and the possible perils of the law. The case still remained under consideration in 1960, and no opinion is ventured here concerning the merits. It involves the International Union of Mine, Mill and Smelter Workers, long regarded as a "left-wing" union. Some years ago it had been expelled from the Congress of Industrial Organizations along with several other labor organizations that were deemed to be too heavily influenced by Communist leaders. Nevertheless, the union continued to represent a number of metals miners and related workers. The officers of the union had sworn that they were not Communists, and the union was legally recognized as bargaining representative for the employees of some important companies. Within the labor movement and among knowing persons, nevertheless, the union was still widely thought to be very "left-wing." Now, by proceeding under the Communist Control Act of 1954, the Attorney General was officially seeking to brand it. It was not necessary for him to show that the nominal leaders of the union were Communists; it would suffice if he could show that there was "effective management" of its affairs by one or more individuals who could be closely tied to the Communist Party. To some observers this seemed a desirable means of revealing not only to the public but to the union members themselves the political links of their organization's managers.

On the other hand, in order to stigmatize the defendant union the statute required more than showing the presence of an effective Communist in the Union's councils. The statute required that the union be "actively engaged in" giving support to the Communist Movement. To establish that branch of his accusation against the Mine, Mill and Smelter Workers, the Attorney General cited a number of actions taken and views espoused by the union. Among them was the union's opposition to the Labor-Management Relations Act of 1947 (the Taft-Hartley Act), the Communist Control Act of 1954, and certain other legislative proposals of an avowedly anti-Communist nature. Now, it is true that these were actively opposed by the Communist Party, which obviously preferred to be free from the harassments and restraints the new laws were likely to bring. But the statutes were energetically fought against as well by a great many non-Communist and, indeed, strongly anti-Communist organizations, including virtually the whole labor movement of the United States, which felt that these measures embodied objectionable and perhaps dangerous policies. To include such things in the proofs of Communist activities is, in effect, to warn all other organizations that opposition to anti-Communist measures may lead to official scrutinizing and,

conceivably, to the charge of "Communist infiltration." Repression of free discussion is almost certainly not the direct objective of the Communist Control Act. But it might well prove to be its achievement, if proceedings under its terms were ever to become frequent.

George Santayana once described fanatics as those who redouble their effort when they have forgotten their goal. Measured by that test, the sponsors of the Communist Control Act came perilously close to the line of fanaticism. Constant concern about the Communist Menace had dulled analysis of its precise nature. As a result, true aim was not always taken when countermeasures against the Menace were being launched. The only legitimate goal of these countermeasures was the preservation of a free society against the threat of totalitarianism. Too often, however, moves have been defended on the ground that they have been directed against Communism, without sufficient attention to the question of whether they have been directed toward Democracy.

The Communist Menace is not in America primarily a matter of ideology. Communist ideas have made little headway in countries that have retained a measure of social mobility, that have developed an equitable economy, and that have been willing to cope with problems rather than simply deny their existence. The need, then, is not to stamp out the expression of communist philosophy. The need is to deal with the actualities of danger. Externally, these are military in character. They must be dealt with by the instruments of diplomacy, by the thrust and counterthrust of power, and eventually by genuine international accord; peaceful coexistence is the only practical alternative to glorious no-existence. Internally, the menace lies in the possibility of espionage, sabotage, or similar activity purposefully related to the supposed interests of a present or potential adversary in the military realm. Clandestine crimes of these types will not be effectively controlled by the mechanisms of registrations, purges, and political purity tests that play a large part in current legislation.

The late Justice Jackson, though concurring in the *Dennis* decision that upheld the constitutionality of the Smith Act, expressed doubt about the long-range effectiveness of efforts to halt Communism by jailing Communists. His words on that occasion have broad significance. "No decision by this Court," he said, "can forestall revolution whenever the existing government fails to command the respect and loyalty of the people, and sufficient distress and discontent is allowed to grow up among the masses. Many failures by fallen governments attest that no government can long prevent revolution by outlawry. Corruption, ineptitude, inflation, oppressive taxation, militarization, injustice, and loss of leadership capable of intellectual initiative in domestic or foreign affairs are allies on which the Communists count to bring opportunity knocking to their door." As these remarks suggest, the true hope of safeguarding democratic institutions against subversion lies in perfecting those institutions, rather than in toying with totalitarian-style weapons.

Suggestions for Additional Reading

Partly because of the Cold War, the Communist Party of the United States of America has probably been studied more thoroughly than the Federalists, the Whigs, the Democrats or the Republicans. Although much of the material published is shoddy and unreliable, some good work has been done. Under the general editorship of Clinton Rossiter, the Fund for the Republic has sponsored a yet unfinished series of books on the CPUSA. Theodore Draper's two volumes, *The Roots of American Communism* (New York, 1957) and *American Communism and Soviet Russia* (New York, 1960) and David Shannon's companion volume, *The Decline of American Communism* (New York, 1959) are all excellent. They provide, except for the period from about 1930 to 1945, the basic history of the CPUSA. For the years not covered by Draper and Shannon—and for additional insights on the years they *do* cover, Irving Howe and Lewis Coser's rather polemical *The American Communist Party* (Boston, 1957) is useful. In the Fund for the Republic series are a number of books on special aspects of "Communism in American Life." Daniel Aaron's *Writers on the Left* (New York, 1961) is especially noteworthy. Also published under auspices of the Fund for the Republic is *Bibliography on the Communist Problem in the United States* (New York, 1955). This bibliography, soon to be brought up-to-date, is excellent. One further title merits mention in this very brief list: Donald Drew Egbert and Stow Persons have edited, in two volumes, *Socialism and American Life* (Princeton, 1952), a massive work which includes relevant essays by Daniel Bell, David Bowers, Will Herberg, Sidney Hook, Paul M. Sweezy, and others. Volume II is devoted to bibliography.

The Communists themselves have seldom failed to recognize the usefulness of agitation and propaganda, for which "agitprop" is their term. Among histories written by members of the CPUSA, Foster's *From Bryan to Stalin* (New York, 1937) and *History of the Communist Party of the United States* (New York, 1952) are useful, as is James Oneal and G. A. Werner's *American Communism* (New York, 1947). The Communists are, however, most effective, from the point of view of a non-Communist, when they move from official histories to autobiographical statements. Among the better known autobiographies are Ella Reeve Bloor, *We are Many* (New York, 1940), Joseph Freeman, *An American Testament* (New York, 1936), and Michael Gold, *Jews Without Money* (New York, 1930). There is also a voluminous literature of autobiographies by *ex*-Communists. Of these, the better known are probably Louis Budenz, *This Is My Story* (New York, 1947); Whittaker Chambers, *Witness* (New York, 1952); and Benjamin Gitlow, *The Whole of Their Lives* (New York, 1948). Less notorious but more reliable are these autobiographies: John Gates, *The Story of an American Communist* (New York, 1958); Granville Hicks, *Where We Came Out* (New York, 1954); and Sandor Voros, *American Commissar* (Philadelphia, 1961).

Students who have access to good libraries will want to move from these relatively available titles to the journals published by the Party or its sympathizers. The liveliest of these are *The Liberator, Masses, New Masses, The Partisan Re-*

view (which quickly moved to an anti-Communist position), and *Masses and Mainstream.* Official and theoretical statements of the Party are usually to be found in *Political Affairs,* which was, before 1944, known as *The Communist.*

The cases reproduced in Part II have, of course, been cut to fit the requirements of space. For example, *The Communist Party v. Subversive Activities Control Board* covers well over 200 pages in its complete version. The *United States Reports* should be consulted by those who wish to read the complete text of the decisions included in this volume. Other related cases well worth the reader's attention are: *Schenck v. United States,* 249 U.S. 47 (1919); *Abrams v. United States,* 250 U.S. 616 (1919); *Gitlow v. New York,* 268 U.S. 652 (1925); *Whitney v. California,* 274 U.S. 357 (1927); *Stromberg v. California,* 283 U.S. 359 (1931); *De Jonge v. Oregon,* 299 U.S. 353 (1937); *Herndon v. Lowry,* 301 U.S. 242 (1937); *Pennsylvania v. Nelson,* 350 U.S. 72 (1956).

For the relationship between Legislative Investigating Committees (Federal and State) and the Courts see, for example: *Watkins v. United States,* 345 U.S. 178 (1957); *Barenblatt v. United States,* 360 U.S. 109 (1959); *Sweezy v. New Hampshire,* 354 U.S. 234 (1959); *Uphaus v. Wyman,* 360 U.S. 72 (1959).

Among the many books on civil liberties and the CPUSA are these: Zechariah Chafee's *The Blessings of Liberty* (Philadelphia, 1956); Walter Gellhorn's *Security, Loyalty and Science* (Ithaca, 1950); Sidney Hook's *Heresy, Yes—Conspiracy, No* (New York, 1953); Herbert Aptheker's *Dare We Be Free?* (New York, 1961); Walter Berns' *Freedom, Virtue and the First Amendment* (Baton Rouge,

1957); Milton R. Konvitz' *Fundamental Liberties of a Free People* (Ithaca, 1957); John Somerville's *The Communist Trials and the American Tradition* (New York, 1956), and Norman Thomas' *The Test of Freedom* (New York, 1954). Alan Barth's *The Loyalty of Free Men* (New York, 1951) remains the best introduction to the problem.

In addition to Aptheker's book, important Communists have published the following: Eugene Dennis, *Letters from Prison* (New York, 1956) and Elizabeth Gurley Flynn et al., *Thirteen Communists Speak to the Court* (New York, 1953). Samuel A. Stouffer's *Communism, Conformity, and Civil Liberties* (New York, 1955) analyzes American attitudes toward dissent.

Periodical literature is endless. Among the more thoughtful articles are these: H. W. Ehrmann, "Zeitgeist and the Supreme Court," *Antioch Review,* XI (December 1951), 424-36; Max Ernst, "Some Affirmative Legislation for a Loyalty Program," *American Scholar,* XIX (October 1950), 452-60; Ernest van den Haag, "Controlling Subversive Groups," *AAAPSS,* CC (July 1955), 62-71; Wallace Mendelson, "Clear & Present Danger—from Schenck to Dennis," *Columbia Law Review,* LII (March 1952), 313-33; Nathaniel Nathanson, "The Communist Trial and the Clear-and-Present Danger Test," *Harvard Law Review,* LXIII (1950), 1167-75; John Somerville, "Law, Logic, and Revolution," *Western Political Quarterly,* XIV (December 1961), 839-49; Arthur E. Sutherland Jr., "Freedom & Internal Security," *Harvard Law Review,* LXIV (1951), 383-416. Alexander D. Brook's *Bibliography on Civil Rights and Liberties in the U.S.* (New York, 1962) is excellent.